"If you want to know the past, look at your present life. If you want to know the future, look at your present."

—GAUTAMA BUDDHA

At three years of age, Joey Verwey of Pretoria, South Africa began talking about her former lives. Her mother, Helge Verwey, started a diary of her recollections— spanning ten lives in all—when she was six years old. Commented South African scientist Dr. Arthur Bleksley: "Before she could write she could draw fashions of ancient times, always supplying the most minute and accurate details. She later described objects, manners and dress that only someone who had lived in the times could possibly know. Her accuracy is uncanny, and other than the possibility that she had indeed been reincarnated several times, I can find no other explanation of her amazing knowledge."

—From "Out of the Mouths of Babes and Sucklings"
The Case for Reincarnation

BANTAM NEW AGE BOOKS

This important imprint includes books in a variety of fields and disciplines and deals with the search for meaning, growth and change. They are books that circumscribe our times and our future. Ask your bookseller for the books you have missed.

BETWEEN HEALTH AND ILLNESS by Barbara B. Brown
THE CASE FOR REINCARNATION by Joe Fisher
THE COSMIC CODE by Heinz R. Pagels
CREATIVE VISUALIZATION by Shakti Gawain
THE DANCING WU LI MASTERS by Gary Zukav
DON'T SHOOT THE DOG: HOW TO IMPROVE YOURSELF
  AND OTHERS THROUGH BEHAVIORAL TRAINING
  by Karen Pryor
ECOTOPIA by Ernest Callenbach
AN END TO INNOCENCE by Sheldon Kopp
ENTROPY by Jeremy Rifkin with Ted Howard
THE FIRST THREE MINUTES by Steven Weinberg
FOCUSING by Dr. Eugene T. Gendlin
GRIST FOR THE MILL by Ram Dass
THE HEART OF HEALING by Bruce Davis and
  Genny Wright Davis
THE HEART OF PHILOSOPHY by Jacob Needleman
HOW TO IMAGINE: A NARRATIVE ON ART AND
  AGRICULTURE by Gianfranco Baruchello and Henry Martin
I CHING: A NEW INTERPRETATION FOR MODERN TIMES
  by Sam Reifler
IF YOU MEET THE BUDDHA ON THE ROAD, KILL HIM!
  by Sheldon Kopp
IN SEARCH OF SCHRÖDINGER'S CAT by John Gribbin
INFINITY AND THE MIND by Rudy Rucker
KISS SLEEPING BEAUTY GOODBYE
  by Madonna Kolbenschlag
THE LIVES OF A CELL by Lewis Thomas
LIVING WITH NUCLEAR WEAPONS
  by Carnesale/Doty/Hoffman/Huntington/Nye and Sagan
MAGICAL CHILD by Joseph Chilton Pearce
THE MEDUSA AND THE SNAIL by Lewis Thomas
MIND AND NATURE by Gregory Bateson
THE MIND'S I by Douglas R. Hofstadter and Daniel C. Dennett
MISSILE ENVY by Dr. Helen Caldicott

MUSIC IN EVERY ROOM: AROUND THE WORLD IN A BAD MOOD by John Krich

MYSTICISM AND THE NEW PHYSICS by Michael Talbot

NEW RULES by Daniel Yankelovich

NEW TECHNOLOGY COLORING BOOK by Rita Aero and Howard Rheingold

ON HUMAN NATURE by Edward O. Wilson

THE ONE-STRAW REVOLUTION by Masanobu Fukuoka

ORDER OUT OF CHAOS by Ilya Prigogine and Isabelle Stengers

PROSPERING WOMAN by Ruth Ross

REENCHANTMENT OF THE WORLD by Morris Berman

SEVEN TOMORROWS by Hawken, Ogilvy and Schwartz

SPACE-TIME AND BEYOND by Bob Toben and Alan Wolf

THE SPHINX AND THE RAINBOW by David Loye

STALKING THE WILD PENDULUM by Itzhak Bentov

STRESS AND THE ART OF BIOFEEDBACK by Barbara B. Brown

SUPERMIND by Barbara B. Brown

THE TAO OF PHYSICS, Revised Edition, by Fritjof Capra

TO HAVE OR TO BE? by Erich Fromm

THE TURNING POINT by Fritjof Capra

THE WAY OF THE SHAMAN: A Guide to Power and Healing by Michael Harner

ZEN AND THE ART OF MOTORCYCLE MAINTENANCE by Robert H. Pirsig

THE ZEN ENVIRONMENT by Marian Mountain

THE CASE FOR REINCARNATION

Joe Fisher

*Preface by His Holiness
The Dalai Lama*

BANTAM BOOKS

TORONTO · NEW YORK · LONDON · SYDNEY · AUCKLAND

THE CASE FOR REINCARNATION

A Bantam Book / published by arrangement with
William Collins and Sons (Canada) Ltd.

PRINTING HISTORY

William Collins and Sons edition published May 1984
Bantam edition / October 1985

To the best of our knowledge the permissions in this book are credited to the correct sources. If there are any errors the publishers would be pleased to correct them in any subsequent edition.

The Pluto transits of Scorpio were determined by Gord Hines of Zodiac House (P.O. Box 5803, Stn. 'A', Toronto, Ontario M5W 1P2) using the DR-70 Astrology Minicomputer by Digicomp Research Corp., Ithaca, N.Y., U.S.A.

New Age and the accompanying figure design as well as the statement "a search for meaning, growth and change" are trademarks of Bantam Books, Inc.

ISBN 0-553-24868-5

Published simultaneously in the United States and Canada

PRINTED IN THE UNITED STATES OF AMERICA

O   0 9 8 7 6 5 4 3

For Reva,
with love.

ཐུགས་རྗེ་ཆེ་གནང་ཅེས།།

OFFICE OF HIS HOLINESS THE DALAI LAMA

Reincarnation is not exclusively a Buddhist or Hindu concept, but is a part of the history of human origin. It stands
as a proof of the mindstream's capacity to retain knowledge of
physical, vocal, and mental activities.

The theory of reincarnation is integral to Tibetan Buddhist
life-style and applies equally to the good and bad mind. It is
related to the theory of interdependent origination and to the law
of cause and effect. It is, therefore, a major factor in the development of that wisdom and compassion ultimately leading to the
attainment of the fully enlightened state of a Buddha.

There are incidents where people, in childhood, recollect and
recognize past life experiences and environments. Furthermore,
a considerable number of scientists are taking keen interest in
the field. Buddhist philosophy can definitely contribute in the
study of mind and its continuum, providing logical modes of
inquiry into the controversial topic of reincarnation.

It is hoped that intensive and sincere comparative study of the
various beliefs regarding reincarnation be carried further in order
that a deeper and more scientific understanding can be conceived.

I am, therefore, happy to introduce this book by Mr. Joe Fisher
and I am sure it will contribute substantially to explain and
interest the average westerner in the subject of rebirth.

October 13, 1983   THE DALAI LAMA

Acknowledgements

The author wishes to express his special thanks to: David Kendall, vintage pal and shadow boxer, for his feral perusal of the manuscript.

Linda Pellowe, for acting so forthrightly on this book's behalf. Brother Malcolm "Laird" Fisher, for his diligence in Sydney, Australia.

Thanks also to Zasep Rinpoche, Tempa Tsering, Tendzin Choegyal, Ian Currie, Peter Commins, Ed Moran, Libby Sellwood, Helen Baltais, Ken Robertson, Kathy Brooks, Larry Kopman, Bill Lanning, Pascal Kaplan, Jim Wheatley, Yuzo Hatano, Cody Poulton, Karl Kamper, Caroline Keenan, Gina Cerminara, Doug Cass, Uwe Ackerman, David Kopman, Faith Brown, Kevin Scanlon, Terri Degler, Al Wainio, Lena McEvenue, Steve Waring, Brian Postnikoff, Alexander Duncan and Patrick Crean for germinating the seed of an idea most timely.

As long as you are not aware of the continual law of
Die and Be Again, you are merely a vague guest on a
dark Earth.

GOETHE

Contents

Preface by His Holiness The Dalai Lama   ix

Foreword   xvii

1 **A Potted History of Rebirth**   1
A summation of reincarnational belief from ancient tribal instinct to the age of technology.

2 **Out of the Mouths of Babes and Sucklings**   5
Garrulous infants are among the most convincing witnesses for rebirth. Spotlight on the work of Dr. Ian Stevenson and Hemendra Banerjee, the world's top reincarnation investigators.

3 **Putting Us in Perspective**   20
Cycles that hinge on rebirth and regeneration are proceeding at every conceivable level of life. Reincarnating humanity is placed in the context of all else that reincarnates—from subatomic particles to the universe.

4 **Prodigies, Plato and Precognition**   25
How the law of rebirth appears to operate independently of heredity and genetics.

5 **Healing the Scars of Centuries**   35
The story of hypnotic regression and past-life therapy. Testimony from leading past-life therapists and documented cases of healing that stems from contact with former existences.

6 **So Long Ago: The Roots of Belief**   51
The primordial origins of belief in rebirth—myth and fable, tribal memory and the great religions of the world.

7 **The Lost Chord of Christianity**   65
How reincarnation was ruthlessly expunged from Christian teaching. Evidence is presented of the rebirth doctrine both in The Bible and The Gnostic Gospels.

8   **The Bardo State: From Grave to Cradle**   76
The plane of consciousness between lives. Testimony of terror, beauty, timelessness and the necessity of self-evaluation.

9   **The Ghost of Future Past**   89
Time as illusion and how it affects the traditionally linear concept of lives strung out one after the other.

10   **Lesser Lives: Rebirth in the Lower Kingdoms**   95
The immense journey of progressive embodiment that comprises the Great Chain of Being. Can humans reincarnate as animals?

11   **Fearless Fighters and the Suicide Fallacy**   109
Warriors who believe in reincarnation are the boldest of fighting men. And those wanting to escape the world by taking their own lives are confounded by the revolving door of rebirth.

12   **Pluto: Planet of Rebirth**   117
As ruler of death and rebirth, Pluto is recognized as a particularly potent force during those rare ages—one every 248 years—when the planet is at large in its own sign of the zodiac, Scorpio. The world is now on the threshold of such an epoch.

13   **The Personal Investigation of Past Lives**   128
How the individual can learn about his or her previous incarnations. Exercises to stimulate the "Magical Memory."

14   **From The Dalai Lama to the Population Conundrum**   144
A miscellany of perspectives on rebirth featuring The Dalai Lama, Edgar Cayce, xenoglossy, déjà vu, past-life artistry and more . . .

15   **Bringing It All Back Home**   159
Assimilating the meaning of reincarnation: the prospect for positive change in the individual and society.

Bibliography   163

Index   173

Foreword

As irrepressible as life itself, reincarnation prevails despite the censure of critics mired in materialism. Tribal societies were nourished by its mythic vigor, classical societies graced the doctrine with logic and reason and twentieth-century societies have tested its scientific validity and revealed its therapeutic power.

Yet the phenomenon of rebirth neither begins nor ends with humans. Everything reincarnates—from subatomic particles to the swirling universe. Even this planet undergoes cycles of death and rebirth. On August 27, 1984, the globe enters a crucial eleven-year astrological age during which Pluto, the planet of rebirth, transits its own sign of Scorpio. This era, which happens only once every 248.4 years, promises, or threatens, to be a period of planetary transformation. Drastic scenarios of nuclear war and geological upheaval vie with, and could possibly precede, the ushering in of long-range peace and unity that characterize the Age of Aquarius.

Scientific proof of reincarnation, it is claimed, is no more than fifteen years away. Some say the day will come when an infant's inventory of past lives can be flashed onto a computer screen as an educational primer, thereby giving parents and child conscious retention of what has gone before in order to enhance the life at hand. Yet scientific proof will never be more convincing than the pilot light which, fueled by the need for rebirth, burns in the human soul.

The Case for Reincarnation, however, will not be relying on subjective testimony. Evidence will be drawn from empirical research, medical assessment, spiritual wisdom, metaphysical investigation, historical record, mystical perception and wide-ranging contemporary experience. The book endeavors to show that knowledge of rebirth expands our vision of who we are as well as granting greater meaning to our role in the universal order.

Because the human race is beleaguered by impending world crises, reincarnation has never appealed so forcefully to the psyche. While well over one billion Asiatics accept rebirth as a fact of life, more and more Westerners are being drawn to enrich their lives through a greater understanding of the ancient wisdom. Many are intrigued, initially, by the revelations of past-life therapy, the research findings of medical professionals and the implications of the so-called new physics. This fascination shows itself in everything from the launching of a California-based magazine devoted exclusively to reincarnation to the sale of tin badges in Britain proclaiming: **Reincarnation Is Making A Comeback.**

"An instinct of the race" is how Henry David Thoreau described the belief that we return to earth in as many fresh embodiments as our spiritual evolution demands. *The Case for Reincarnation* defines and explains this instinct, and pursues its significance for modern humanity.

1

A Potted History of Rebirth

The tomb is not a blind alley; it is a thoroughfare. It closes on the twilight. It opens on the dawn.

VICTOR HUGO

Every new-born being indeed comes fresh and blithe into the new existence, and enjoys it as a free gift: but there is, and can be, nothing freely given. Its fresh existence is paid for by the old age and death of a worn-out existence which has perished, but which contained the indestructible seed out of which this new existence has arisen: they are one being.

ARTHUR SCHOPENHAUER

For our ancestors, going to the grave was to return to Mother Earth with her boundless capacity for rebirth. To die was to be reborn, and to be reborn was to be physically refitted so as to express, more appropriately, deathless spiritual energy. Chuang Tzu, the Taoist mystic who lived in the fourth century before Christ, captured the optimism of the process when he wrote: "To have attained to the human form

1

must be always a source of joy. And then, to undergo count-less transitions, with only the infinite to look forward to—what incomparable bliss is that!"

As civilization slowly evolved from a scattered tribal lifestyle, primal instincts of renewal, which had inspired sacred myth and lent meaning to the rigors of day-to-day survival, became the doctrine of reincarnation. And the doctrine's professed rationale for everyone's succession of Earth lives is karma; the notion that whatever a person thinks and does acts upon the equilibrium of the universe to create its own reaction. In other words, rebirth never lets up until all imperfection has been eradicated through the complex inter-play of cause and effect. Karma's impersonal justice is implicit in the very fabric of the universe. The law of the conservation of energy which decrees that no energy is ever lost, Newton's third law of motion (every action has its reaction which is equal and opposite) and the oft-quoted Biblical phrase: "What-soever a man soweth, that shall he also reap" (Galations 6:7) all testify to karmic accountancy.

Since the espousal of reincarnation and karma by the wisest spiritual and philosophical sages, the people of the East have remained in awe of the relentless revolutions of the "wheel of life." Not so their counterparts in the Western Hemisphere where reincarnation was buried alive more than fourteen centuries ago. The conspiring undertakers were the church and the state, fearful that their authority could be challenged by a doctrine that made individuals responsible for their own salvation. Since A.D. 553, when the "monstrous restoration" of rebirth was denounced by Emperor Justinian, the faithful have been taught to believe in eternal life while ignoring immortality's spiritual sister, reincarnation. Chris-tians learn that eternity starts at birth. But, since only the beginningless can be endless, one might as well have faith in a table's ability to stand on only three legs!

Such quasi-immortality rendered materialism more at-tractive as a code by which to live. Consequently, with the growth of Western materialism indirectly ordained by the church, reincarnation's exile was confirmed. For materialism, which later bound fledgling science to its blinkered vision, sanctions no reality outside that which can be measured, weighed, heard, smelled, bought and sold. Ironically, this trend also hastened the decline of ecclesiastical authority, which relied largely on the manipulation of the intangible.

The church was to remain all-powerful for centuries, even as it carried the seeds of its own decay. Many a rebel reincarnationist was put to death with vengeful fury as the bishops implicitly condemned the rebirth doctrine twice more at the councils of 1274 and 1439 with thunderous assertions about heaven, purgatory and hell. Yet the ancient belief that many lives are as essential to our spiritual evolution as a succession of years are to our physical development wouldn't be stamped out. When the Dark Ages retreated before the Renaissance, society was reborn in a spontaneous exaltation of individuality. The hold of the papacy was finally broken and, in the Age of Enlightenment that followed, many of the great minds of Europe vented the conviction that reincarnation was an unalterable fact of life which tempered the chaos of an unfair world with justice, meaning and purpose. "After all," noted Voltaire, "it is no more surprising to be born twice than it is to be born once."

The masses, however, had other things to be surprised about as tremendous excitement was being generated by the rudimentary automation of the industrial revolution. Towards the end of the last century, the Theosophical movement challenged the prevailing mechanism of the times by rummaging around in the treasure chest of Hindu and Buddhist observance to retrieve reincarnation for adoption in the West. Pickled in fundamentalist concepts and skewered by the fear of death with its stark remuneration of either paradise or hellfire, most people weren't to be swayed.

Our own century witnessed the limited response, in the 1930s and 1940s, to the God-fearing mystic Edgar Cayce, who went into self-hypnotic trance to deliver—at first against his own wishes—startling revelations about past lives extending all the way back to the lost continent of Atlantis.

Not until the Bridey Murphy sensation of 1954 did the public imagination accept reincarnation as a reasonable hypothesis. Believers and unbelievers alike were captivated by accounts of how Colorado businessman Morey Bernstein had hypnotically regressed housewife Virginia Tighe to an obscure but historically plausible life in last-century Ireland as Bridey Murphy. Reincarnation-inspired movies and songs followed. So did pioneering studies that subjected past-life recall to scientific scrutiny. As files of intriguing cases grew, the mid-seventies saw past-life therapy emerge as a dramatic way of curing physical and psychological disorders through the tapping of reincarnational memories under hypnosis. Belief in successive lives was not, however, enjoying its rebirth in isolation. Rather, it was taking place amid a widespread resurgence of spiritual awareness and a developing hunger for nonmaterial nourishment in what had become a highly technological world.

In 1982, the Gallup poll organization announced that very nearly one American in four believed in reincarnation. Three years earlier, a *Sunday Telegraph* poll had reported the same belief was held by 28 per cent of all British adults—an increase of 10 per cent in ten years. And in 1980, 29 per cent of 1,314 people responding to a questionnaire in the ultra-conservative London *Times* attested to a belief in reincarnation.

Skeptics, of course, have never stopped sniping at the "credulous" types who ascribe so many of life's insights and idiosyncracies to echoes of other lives. They dismiss the host of past-life claims as spirit possession, extrasensory perception or tricks played by the mind which we do not fully understand. Nevertheless, reincarnation continues to divest itself of the banishment so long imposed by the trinity of church, state and scientific materialsim. In the words of Austrian scientist and educator Rudolf Steiner: ". . . Just as an age was once ready to receive the Copernican theory of the universe, so is our own age ready for the ideas of reincarnation and karma to be brought into the general consciousness of humanity. And what is destined to happen in the course of evolution *will* happen, no matter what powers rise up against it."

2

Out of the Mouths of Babes and Sucklings

. . . The most promising evidence bearing on rein-carnation seems to come from the spontaneous cases, especially among children.

IAN STEVENSON

Have you never observed that children will some-times, of a sudden, give utterance to ideas which makes us wonder how they got possession of them, which presuppose a long series of other ideas and secret self-communings, which break forth like a full stream out of the earth, an infallible sign that the stream was not produced in a moment from a few raindrops, but had long been flowing concealed be-neath the ground . . . ?

J. G. HERDER

Spontaneously, in scattered remarks mixed with mundane chatter about the world around her, little Romy Crees poured out her memories of the man she insisted she once was. As soon as she could talk, the pretty, curly haired toddler from Des Moines, Iowa said she was Joe Williams, husband of Sheila and father of three children. Again and again, she expressed the wish to "go home." Then she went on to describe her death in a motorcycle accident, a description so graphic that her parents were jolted into taking seriously what they had at first dismissed as the drivelings of childhood fantasy. "I'm afraid of motorcycles," said Romy.

So persistent were the three-year-old's "memories" of incidents and personalities from this other, mysterious life that her parents eventually agreed to a visit from Hemendra Banerjee, a professional investigator of "extracerebral memory." Accompanied by his wife and research associate, Margit, and two journalists from the Swedish magazine *Allers*, Banerjee arrived at the Crees' home on a cold winter's day in 1981. Her curls dancing about her rosy face, Romy was playing energetically on the living room's thick broadloom in a blue floral dress. A Roman Catholic image of the Madonna smiled down from the wall as Bonnie Crees, twenty-eight, told how she had tried to distract her daughter, hoping to deflect these disturbing recollections while encouraging more normal conversation. But still the other life intruded . . .

"I went to school in Charles City," Romy would say. "I lived in a red brick house and I married Sheila and we had children, but we did not live in Charles City then . . ."

"Mother has a pain in her leg—here," she said, pointing to her right leg. "Mother Williams' name is Louise. I haven't seen her for a long time."

"When I lived at home there was a fire. It was my fault, but mother threw water on the fire. She burnt her hand."

Romy's face lit up with concern as Bonnie Crees related her daughter's preoccupation with Joe Williams and Charles City. "I want to go to Charles City," she declared. "I must tell Mother Williams that everything is O.K."

So it was that the Banerjees, the Swedish journalists, Des Moines specialist Dr. Greg States and Barry Crees set off with Romy for Charles City, a town of 8,000 people some 140 miles away. For the entire journey, Romy was restless and excitable, and as Charles City was approached—without a word from anyone as to the imminence of their destination—she climbed over from the back seat to squeeze between Dr. States and Hemendra Banerjee. "We have to buy flowers," she said. "Mother Williams loves blue flowers. And when we get there we can't go in through the front door. We have to go around the corner to the door in the middle."

Because Romy was uncertain of Mrs. Williams' address in this modern town of churches and bungalows set among spreading fields close to the Minnesota border, the party consulted the local telephone directory. Soon they arrived, not at a red brick house as they had been led to suppose from Romy's earlier statement, but at a white bungalow on the outskirts of town. There, Romy jumped out of the car and pulled Banerjee impatiently up the path that led to the front door and a printed notice: PLEASE USE THE BACK DOOR.

There was no initial response to the ringing of the doorbell, but at last the back door was opened wearily by an elderly woman leaning on metal crutches. Romy's words about "a pain in her leg" were as accurate as her prediction about the front door. For around the right leg of the old woman—who was indeed Mrs. Louise Williams—was a tightly wrapped bandage. Mrs. Williams, however, was about to leave for an appointment with her doctor and wanted neither to talk to the group nor hear their stories. She closed the door, and Romy's eyes filled with tears.

Romy, her father and the Swedish journalists returned an hour later and were received into the home. There was immediate rapport between Romy and the old lady and kisses and hugs were shared as Mrs. Williams accepted and unwrapped Romy's gift of flowers. Bemused by her visitors and astonished at Romy's choice of bouquet, Mrs. Williams disclosed that her late son's last gift had been a posy of blue flowers. She was even more astonished when Barry Crees, who was also wrestling with disbelief, related Romy's collected reminiscences about the Williams family. "Where did this girl get all this information?" Mrs. Williams wanted to know. "I don't know you or anyone else in Des Moines." The seventy-six-year-old woman then explained why she was living in a white bungalow and why the community must have appeared strange to Romy, even with her uncanny familiarity. "Our house was made of red brick," she said, "but it was destroyed in an awful tornado that damaged much of Charles City ten years ago. Joe helped us build this house and insisted we keep the front door shut in winter."

Mrs. Williams broke off her narrative to shuffle into the next room and Romy rushed after her. Later, they returned, holding hands. Little Romy appeared to be trying to support the old woman who was clutching a framed photograph of Joe, Sheila and the children taken the Christmas before the accident. "She recognized them," murmured Mrs. Williams, incredulously. "She recognized them!"

Joe's marriage to Sheila, the three children that followed, the names of other relatives, the 1975 motorcycle accident near Chicago in which Joe and Sheila were killed, the fire at home where Mrs. Williams burned her hand: these and other details mentioned by Romy were all confirmed. Her precise description of the injuries sustained in the fatal accident was also found to be accurate. Born in 1937, Joe Williams, who died two years before Romy was born, was the second youngest of seven children.

The case of Romy Crees is the best-documented study in Banerjee's files and, according to the investigator, "demonstrates that reincarnation is real." But as devout Catholics, Romy's parents and Louise Williams couldn't bring themselves to accept that explanation. "I don't know how to explain it," sighed Bonnie Crees, "but I *do* know my daughter isn't lying."

Hankering for Past Lives

Romy is just one of hundreds of young children from all parts of the world who had spoken volubly, accurately and with unswerving conviction about previous lives that have been historically verified. In most cases, these guileless witnesses voice their memories between the ages of two and five years, telling, usually, of lives that ended abruptly and with violence. Muttering distractedly or pleading to be heard, they use such phrases as: "When I was big," and have been known to grumble about the limitations of their small bodies and even to speak resentfully of not being the same sex as before. Often they yearn for the lost companionship of a husband, wife, son or daughter. They hanker for the food, clothing and lifestyle—even, on occasion, the alcohol, drugs or tobacco—of a former existence. They suffer phobias that can be linked directly with their unexpected deaths—sharp knives, perhaps, or motor vehicles, or water. Yet these small children have little hope of neutralizing such powerful impulses because they are rarely encouraged to air their past-life memories. In the West, parents tend to dismiss and deflect what they consider to be nonsensical ramblings, while in the East, there's a superstition that those who remember a previous existence are fated to die young. In India, southern Asia and Turkey it is not uncommon for parents to react by filling their child's mouth with filth or soap.

Railway clerk B. Ram Ghulam Kapoor may have been too dumbfounded to reach for the soap dish when his five-year-old son, Bishen Chand, launched into a man-to-man chat about sex. "Papa," Bishen wondered aloud one day, "why don't you keep a mistress? You will have great pleasure from her." Managing to conceal his amazement, his father asked quietly: "What pleasure, my boy?" To which Bishen replied: "You will enjoy the fragrance of her hair and feel much joy from her company."

Bishen's memories, recorded in Bareilly, Uttar Pradesh, India in the mid-1920s, were found to correspond with the life of Laxmi Narain, who had died in 1918 at the age of thirty-two in Shahjahanpur, Uttar Pradesh. The only son of a wealthy landowner, Laxmi had overindulged himself in food, clothes, women and alcohol and had cherished a prostitute by the name of Padma.

When Bishen was twenty-three years old and working in the central excise office at Tenakpore, Padma, then fifty-two, happened to walk across the threshold. Bishen recognized her at once and was so overcome with emotion that he fainted. That evening, he set out for Padma's home with the intent of renewing the relationship Laxmi had enjoyed more than twenty-six years earlier. As Laxmi would have done, Bishen approached the house carrying a bottle of wine even though he was a teetotaller. Padma was not amused. She smashed the wine bottle and sent him back into the night saying: "I am an old woman like your mother."

In 1971, Bishen Chand told psychiatrist Dr. Ian Stevenson, of the University of Virginia, that he had never drunk alcohol before or since this occasion. But the intensity of his aroused affection for Padma left him eager to abandon his abstemious ways.

"He Killed Me"

There are exceptions, however, to the fondness most subjects feel for past-life personalities, and none is more dramatic than the way Reena Gupta reacted to the last man in her life. When Reena was less than two years old she told her grandmother: "I have a *gharwala* (husband). My *gharwala* was a very bad man. He killed me."

Reena's behavior was as bizarre as her utterances. She would toddle out onto the balcony of her New Delhi home and stare into the street crowds; searching, always searching. When out in the family car, she was perpetually on the lookout for someone. "I'm looking for my *gharwala* and my children," she would tell anyone who asked what she was up to. Reena's strangeness became exasperating when she began to criticize the way her mother cooked and did chores around the house. It wasn't long before Reena, who claimed to have four youngsters of her own, wandered off during a market outing only to explain later to her worried mother that she had followed a woman "who used to come to my house." The past-life connection wouldn't go away and, to her mother's annoyance, the little girl continued to express affection for her children as well as anguish at her enforced separation from them. Mercifully, the explanation that this double life demanded was on the way. Vijendra Kaur, a teaching colleague of Reena's mother, had heard about a Sikh family in another part of the city that had suffered in a way that seemed to tally with Reena's stories. Her enquiries, conducted five years after Reena had first spoken of her past life, led to the door of Sardar Kishan Singh and his wife, parents of the late Gurdeep Kaur, who had been murdered by her husband on June 2, 1961. Intrigued by a possible link with their dead daughter, the couple called on the Gupta family. Reena was fast asleep but, on waking, she looked up at the Singhs and her face became all smiles as she said: "They are my father and mother."

The next day, the Singhs brought Swarna, Gurdeep's

younger sister, to see Reena who immediately called her by her nickname, Sarno. In India, custom decrees that gifts of money may be accepted only by a person younger than the giver. So Reena's response was particularly revealing when Swarna offered her two rupees. "How can I take money from Sarno?" she said. "She is younger than me." Later, Reena visited Kishan Singh's home where she recognized as herself a photograph of the late Gurdeep Kaur.

It was only a matter of time before Surjeet Singh, the husband and killer of Gurdeep, heard of Reena's claims and was drawn to pay a visit of his own. Reena, however, had no wish to see him. "He will kill me again," she said, clearly unenthusiastic that Surjeet Singh, once jailed for life for murdering his wife and her brother, had been freed after ten years because of good behavior. When they met in 1975, Reena was nine years old and all the good behavior in the world would not have been enough to allay her fears. Only with the greatest reluctance would she pose—perching uneasily on the armrest of Surjeet Singh's chair—with the man she is convinced was her murderer. In fact, when Surjeet Singh tried to put his arms around her, she tore herself away. But when Reena met Gurdeep Kaur's four children—three daughters and one son—she greeted them as joyfully as she had Gurdeep's mother, father and sister.

Spontaneous Emotional Recognition

Without doubt, young children are the best witnesses to reincarnation. They have yet to be distracted by the information barrage and the crowded memories of later years. Their lack of worldly experience makes them, if not incorruptible, much less inclined to fraudulence than adults. And although parental manipulation can never be ruled out, it's practically impossible to fake the strong identification so commonly felt with the former personality, or the powerful emotional attachment expressed towards surviving past-life relatives and friends. As Banerjee says: "To witness spontaneous emotional recognition is what convinces me more than anything of a case's validity." In the facilitation of such recognition, there often appears to be another factor at work, something Banerjee describes as "the geography of reincarnation." Studies indicate that those whose lives have ended prematurely tend to return to the same general area, drawn back, one can surmise, by a sense of unfinished business and emotional hunger.

Nevertheless, the casebooks of spontaneous past-life memories, well-stocked and painstakingly researched though they may be, cannot prove reincarnation. And they never will. It's no accident that Dr. Ian Stevenson always refers to even his best cases as being "suggestive" of reincarnation. He writes: "All of the cases I have investigated so far have some flaws, many of them serious ones. Neither any single case nor all of the investigated cases together offer anything like a proof of reincarnation. They provide instead a body of evidence suggestive of reincarnation that appears to be accumulating in amount and quality."

Even when a link with a past life is established beyond doubt and in the most precise detail, nobody can *prove* that the child with all the emotion and information was once the person he or she claims to be. Besides, the possibility will always exist that the youngster's memory could have been encouraged by fraud, extrasensory perception, spirit possession or cryptomnesia, that is, the welling up of forgotten memory originating in the present life. Yet these alternative interpretations are, in Stevenson's opinion, "just as mind-stretching as is reincarnation itself, at least for most Westerners."

Spirit possession is perhaps the most likely rival to reincarnation, but even this theory appears decidedly anaemic when birthmark evidence is taken into consideration. Stevenson has examined well over 200 birthmarks on children claiming to have been killed by bullets and bladed weapons that had pierced the corresponding part of their anatomy in a previous life. In seventeen such cases, medical documents such as hospital records or autopsy reports have been obtained that establish that the past-life individual was killed in the way described.

As the case of William George Jr. attests, violence is not a necessary component of birthmark evidence. Although this case has the air of a tribal folk tale, Stevenson has meticulously documented the evidence by personally interviewing, on separate occasions, family members, relatives and friends.

It all started when William George Sr., a celebrated fisher-man of the Tlingit Indian tribe of Alaska, made a vow when he began to doubt the tribe's traditional belief in reincarnation. "If there is anything to this rebirth business," he told his favorite son, Reginald George, "I will come back and be your son." He could be recognized, he said, by the half-inch birthmarks he possessed—one on the left shoulder, the other on the left forearm. Furthermore, he handed over his gold watch with the promise of regaining it should there be another incarnation.

Soon afterwards, the old man was lost at sea and, barely nine months later—on May 5, 1950—Susan George gave birth to her ninth child. The baby was born with two distinctive birthmarks in identical locations to those of his grandfather, though half their size. There was no debate over the baby's name: they called him William George Jr.

Friends and relatives were quick to notice how similar the little boy was to his grandfather. Not only did he look like a diminutive version of the old man, he also walked like him and demonstrated a precocious knowledge of fishing and boats, even while showing more fear of the water than was usual for boys of his age. He called his great aunt "sister," referred to his uncles and aunts as his sons and daughters and didn't object when his own brothers and sisters called him "grandfather." At four years of age, after wandering into his parents' bedroom where Susan George was sorting through her jewelry box, William spied the gold watch that had belonged to William George Sr. "That's my watch," he declared, picking it up. Eventually, the boy grudgingly surrendered ownership. Even though his past-life memories faded in later childhood, he never renounced his claim to "my watch."

Sexual Confusion

Obsession with an existence that has gone before can lead to confusion over sexual identity. Two girls who were sure they were male in former existences—Dolan Mitra of West Bengal and Ma Tin Aung Myo of Upper Burma—insisted, year after year, on wearing boys' clothes and playing boys' games. Dolan, who was born on August 8, 1967, started donning her elder brother's clothes at three years of age and, as she grew older, liked nothing better than to play football and cricket. Thinking she would spoil her brother's clothes, her mother, Konika Mitra, was quick to scold the little girl who replied that she used to be a bigger boy who lived in Burdwan, a community seventy-five miles from her home in Narendrapur. This claim was seen to be justified after Dolan's parents finally agreed to take her to Burdwan, if only to end her crying and distress. Although the first visit, in October, 1971, failed to locate Dolan's former home, a second attempt in March, 1972, was thoroughly successful. Starting from a local landmark, the Annapurna Temple, Dolan led the way through twisty streets to the home of Anath Saran Dey where she was invited in by Dey's youngest daughter, Rita. Dolan scampered knowingly through the house recognizing rooms, and identifying their contents, and then proceeded to point out the possessions of Rita's late brother, Nishith, a student and keen sportsman who had died, supposedly of a brain tumor, in a Calcutta hospital on July 25, 1964. Dolan also recognized Nishith's mother among a group of women and, in subsequent recognition tests, correctly identified a number of relatives and friends.

Ma Tin Aung Myo's male memory made an even deeper impression. Born in 1953, she first experienced the shadow of the past as a four-year-old: she had started to cry when an airplane flew over while she was out walking with her father. Thereafter, a passing plane would always make her cower and weep. When reproached about her behavior she would say: "What do you know? I was shot and killed." She began to tell how, as a Japanese soldier stationed in the family's village of Na-Thul during the last war, she had been strafed by an Allied plane. She remembered wearing short pants and a big belt. And she recalled having taken off her shirt in readiness to cook a meal when the aircraft dived, spraying bullets. As she grew up, Ma Tin Aung Myo expressed a longing to return to Japan to see her wife and children, was adamant about wearing boys' clothes and enjoyed playing at being a soldier. At twelve years of age, she dropped out of school when the authorities demanded that she dress in girls' clothes. By the age of nineteen she had rejected her sex completely. Continuing to dress in male garb, she had no desire for a husband but, instead, said she wanted to marry a girl.

By the age of ten, memories of previous existences have usually evaporated in the heat of life like some strange cerebral mist. But by then the extraordinary behavior of the formative years will have taken its toll. The perplexity and anguish generated by infantile yearning for a different lifestyle in another location certainly does nothing to foster harmony between parent and child. And though many parents manage to resist emotional pressure from their offspring to visit another set of relatives, children have been known to retaliate by running off to the other home they seem to know so well.

Psychologist Dr. Helen Wambach of San Francisco is against encouraging children to recall past-life memories because she believes that such "premature immersion" only adds needlessly to the burden of adjustment in the present life. She vividly remembers an experience in psychotherapy—long before her involvement in reincarnation research—when she was treating a five-year-old called Peter for hyperactivity. To her astonishment, the boy launched into a monologue about his life as a policeman. At first, Dr. Wambach thought Peter must be relating some episode that he had seen on television, but the more he talked the more she understood that he was reliving experiences he felt had been his own. The boy's mother revealed that he had started to speak about his life as a cop at three years of age but she had told him "not to make up stories." Dr. Wambach, on the other hand, enjoyed listening to Peter's tales of law and order—until his mother reported that a policeman had brought him home because he was out in the middle of the street trying to direct traffic. "I felt slightly guilty," Dr. Wambach confessed, "because he had told me about his traffic assignment in his life as a policeman and apparently was beginning to act out his past-life recall—worrisome behavior for a five-year-old."

Worrisome also describes the way a two-year-old boy from Waukomis, Oklahoma, insisted his name was Jimmy. "No, it's Jeremy," he would be told. ". . . Your name is Jeremy Anderson."

Leafing through a picture book with his grandmother, Nancy Anderson, Jeremy spotted a wagon and, in so doing, offered another clue to his predicament which went unnoticed at the time. "He told me the wagon hit him," his grandmother recalled. "He said he was dead, and he was angry with the man who drove the wagon. I didn't think any more about it." On another occasion, when Jeremy's grandfather, Jack, was resting in bed with a bad back, he had asked: "What's wrong with your back, Papa? Is it killing you?" Jack replied that while his back hurt, it wasn't exactly "killing him." And Jeremy said: "Well, my back got hurt one time and it killed me."

All this time a gravestone bearing the name of James L. Houser (August 22, 1952–August 12, 1967) had been standing 90 miles away in a cemetery at Tonkawa, Oklahoma. "Jimmy" Houser, as he was known, was the son of Nancy Anderson and the half-brother of Ron Anderson, Jeremy's father. He was raised by his paternal grandmother in Tonkawa. Jimmy was last seen alive on a broiling August day just ten days short of his fifteenth birthday. A police accident report states that Jimmy Houser, fourteen, and his pal Kevin Lucas, sixteen, were driving at 75 m.p.h. in a Buick sedan with Lucas at the wheel when they struck a truck at a rural intersection. The car skidded 99 feet before bouncing off a second truck and spinning a further 108 feet. Kevin Lucas, who is said to have no memory of the accident or his life before the accident, was seriously injured. Jimmy was killed.

In April, 1980, when Jeremy was five years of age, he was taken to the scene of the accident. Apparently recognizing his surroundings, he became quite emotional and went on to demonstrate how he had fallen out of the car. "I was going like a bullet," he said. "It was like a bomb." Jeremy wasn't surprised when the undertaker who had examined Jimmy's body later disclosed that the corpse had been marked by the type of injuries normally sustained by a driver rather than a passenger. Jeremy, you see, has always insisted he *was* the driver.

Two-Year-Old Pilot

Why, then, are these remarkable children alone in their awareness of a previous existence? Dr. Stevenson suggests that the relatively low incidence of past-life recall doesn't necessarily mean that rebirth is restricted to garrulous infants. Reincarnation could be a much more widespread phenomenon with many people retaining only very dim impressions that would need stimulating—perhaps through encounters with certain people or places—to bring them into the conscious mind. *Déjà vu* experiences, so prevalent among adults and children alike, can be explained thus as the activation of the imprint of past-life memory. The same can be said for certain types of dreams.

Dreams and *déjà vu* can provide dramatic personal pointers to a former life. But spontaneous infant testimony, unsullied by self-consciousness or social conditioning, goes much further by carrying the reincarnational suggestion out of the individual mind and into the public domain. Only the most skeptical can fail to wonder about reincarnation when a boy called Ramu, aged only two years and nine months but already inordinately fond of helicopters, is able to give precise, gestured directions to a pilot of the Indian Air Force in the flying of his machine. Only the most insensitive would belittle the screams of another two-year-old, this time in Toronto, who became panic-stricken at the sight of closing elevator doors. "Don't be silly. It won't kill you," his mother told him. "It did before," the child replied.

Traversing the wide world beyond the cradle to collect, test and collate the past-life tales of toddlers has practically convinced Dr. Ian Stevenson and Hemendra Banerjee that reincarnation is a fact of life. For Banerjee, the irresistible conclusion came after twenty-four years of research. "I'm always finding loopholes and always asking if there is another way to explain the phenomena," he says. "Cumulatively, however, there are patterns in the cases that have made me believe in reincarnation." Stevenson is, by nature, more detached and intellectually austere than Banerjee. But even this shy, circumspect professional goes so far as to say that "a rational man can, if he wants now, believe in reincarnation on the basis of evidence rather than simply on the basis of religious doctrine or cultural tradition."

To accept this evidence is to regard all children with new interest and respect. For if a moral emerges from the mouths of these remarkable babes and sucklings it is that infants should be looked upon less and less as the creations and constructions of their parents, and more and more as people for whom the family is merely a setting for their most recent stage of personal development.

The Investigators

Infant claims of past-life memory from Alaska to Zaire have lured Dr. Ian Stevenson and Hemendra Banerjee around the world countless times. Although practically alone in their calling, they have little in common. In fact, these two men, who for more than two decades have pioneered scientific study into childhood memory that defies ordinary understanding, could scarcely be more different.

Based in Los Angeles, Banerjee, fifty-three, is short, plump, dark-skinned and outgoing, even publicity-hungry. Stevenson, sixty-five, Carlson Professor of Psychiatry at the University of Virginia, is tall, lean, fair-skinned and reserved. Although they once worked together, personal and professional acrimony has separated them since 1964.

Assisted by a team of researchers, Stevenson has more than 2,000 child cases filed on computer at his Department of Parapsychology. Banerjee, helped only by his wife and research associate, Margit, has gathered more than 1,100 cases since 1955 when a university professor in his native India told him: "You will ruin your career this way." "Twenty years ago," Banerjee admits, "people would not touch me with a big bamboo." Even today, with reincarnation still a sensitive, controversial topic, he must contend with the scientific establishment's unrelenting exclusion. The books he writes on the subject are aimed at the popular market while Stevenson's literary output is more staid and scholarly in style and presentation. Founder of the Indian Institute of Parapsychology in 1957, Banerjee has been living in the United States since 1970. As a researcher, he says he acts like a detective, lawyer and psychologist rolled into one, his aim being "to create a body of data so that serious-minded people can make up their minds about reincarnation for themselves—from the evidence."

Montreal-born Stevenson, whose work has been published in the prestigious *Journal of Nervous and Mental*

Disease, says that "dissatisfaction with modern theories of personality" fuels his investigative persistence. Reincarnation, he feels, could account for certain behavior not explained by genetics and early environmental influences. Dr. Harold Lief, a friend and admirer of Stevenson, describes him as a methodical, careful, even cautious, investigator with a personality inclined towards obsessiveness. "Either he is making a colossal mistake," Lief has written, "or he will be known as the Galileo of the twentieth century."

3

Putting Us in Perspective

Reincarnation is implicit in the manifested universe and is a basic and fundamental theme underlying systemic pulsation.

ALICE A. BAILEY

Are not all things which have opposites generated out of their opposites?

SOCRATES

There is inhalation, there is exhalation; there is death, there is rebirth. Such is the drama of continuity that sustains the all-pervading process in which we are enveloped. As the catalyst of transformation on which the evolution of all matter and spirit depends, reincarnation is ceaselessly within us and around us. From the tiniest micro to the macro most huge, cycles that hinge on rebirth and regeneration are proceeding at every conceivable level of life.

The idea of palingenesis (a word of Greek and Latin origin literally meaning "again, birth") is as old as the human race. Eastern mystics have long viewed the universe in terms of *samsara*, or continuous death and rebirth. Shiva, the four-armed Hindu god of creation and destruction, symbolizes this vision by performing the dance of the cosmos through endless cycles of rise and fall, wax and wane. In ancient China, the *Tao*—meaning the very nature of the life process—was seen to be expressed by relentless cycles of coming and going. The universe swung backwards and forwards between *yin* and *yang*. The rational West, trussed for centuries in a strait-jacket tailored by scientific concepts that impeded any meeting of matter and spirit, looked condescendingly upon this exotic interpretation. Until, that is, science was pushed into a magnificent transformation of its own perceptions. The transformation was triggered by Einstein's theories of relativity which showed there was much more to time, space and motion in the universe than classical Newtonian physics had allowed. Next came the development of quantum mechanics and its rigorous inquiry into the nature of subatomic phenomena. Imagine the furrowed brows of the old world eggheads when, like a gorgeous butterfly emerging from an earthbound cocoon, this so-called new physics of the twentieth century made the breathtaking discovery that subatomic particles, from which all matter is made, are indeed partaking in the relentless choreography of death and rebirth. Writes Gary Zukav in the *The Dancing Wu Li Masters*:

> Every subatomic interaction consists of the annihilation of the original particles and the creation of new subatomic particles. The subatomic world is a continual dance of creation and annihilation, of mass changing to energy and energy changing to mass. Transient forms sparkle in and out of existence creating a never-ending, forever-newly-created reality.

In other words, science advances the hypothesis that a microscopic form of rebirth underlies everything in the physical world. In *The Tao Of Physics* Fritjof Capra refers to these subatomic particles as being "destructible and indestructible at the same time." This is precisely what is implied by reincarnation: even as we die we are capable of activating another body. Destructible yet indestructible. Dead yet very much alive.

A similar process is taking place among the fifty trillion cells in the human body. At a rate that defies imagination, old cells perish and new ones are created from a mixture of the dead material and freshly absorbed nutrients. Every second, two million oxygen-carrying red cells are dying and being replaced while the hundreds of millions of cells in the human gut renew themselves completely every one or two days. Tracer studies have shown that, in the course of a year, approximately 98 per cent of the atoms in the human body are replaced by other atoms ingested with air, food and drink. While the origins of this infinitesimal exchange are lost in the prehistoric mysteries of evolution, Colin Wilson argues in his work *The Occult* that true evolution didn't begin until life managed to overcome its most basic problem of forgetfulness. Progress became possible only when the life force invented the trick of coding knowledge into the reproductory processes. He writes:

> The Pre-Cambrian creatures shed old cells and grew new ones in the same way that my body replaces all its old cells every eight years. With the invention of death and reproduction, *they shed old bodies and grew new ones.* . . . Life is not at the mercy of death. It is in control of death. Half a billion years ago, it learned the secret of reincarnation.

Shooting far beyond the body into the vastness of space, the same principle appears to be at work in the most macroscopic of worlds. While agreeing to disagree on the finer points of theory, many cosmologists and astro-physicists suggest the universe is oscillating, forever dying in order to be reborn. Big Bang is followed by expansion followed by collapse into another fireball ripe for explosion. Renowned astrophysicist John Gribbin says he believes the universe "rolls on forever in an eternal cycle in which death is merely the necessary prelude to rebirth."

Recent developments in high-energy astro-physics have led to speculation that the stuff of the universe doesn't vanish into enormous *cul-de-sacs* when sucked into black holes, but is pumped out again on the far side into white holes or quasars. In this way, universes can feed endlessly on one another using black holes as colossal uterine tracts of transformation. Such a recycling of the cosmos was described in picture language in the Bible long before the stirrings of the scientific age. St. Paul, in his epistle to the Hebrews (1:10–12), says that the earth and heavens "all shall wax old as doth a garment. And as a vesture shalt thou fold them up, and they shall be changed." Earlier still, human rebirth was similarly likened to a change of clothes in the great Hindu scripture, the Bhagavad-Gita (2:17): ". . . As a man casting off worn-out garments, taketh new ones, so the dweller in the body, casting off worn-out bodies, entereth into others that are new. . . ."

In the sixteenth century, visionary Italian philosopher Giordano Bruno had the audacity to champion the heretical Copernican theory of the sun-centred solar system as well as the doctrine of reincarnation. To Bruno, rebirth was at the heart of the ubiquitous emanation and return of the "Life of the Universe," embracing atoms, human beings and worlds. He spoke of the circulation of the blood as reflecting the cosmic scheme and taught that circular movement is the only enduring form of motion. Furthermore, he declared that the planet Earth has a soul and maintained that every part of the globe—mineral as well as plant, animal and human—is animated by the same elemental soul matter, there being no distinction between what is terrestrial and what is celestial. As a Catholic, Bruno agreed that souls do not pass from body to body, but go to Paradise, Purgatory or Hell. "But I have reasoned deeply," he wrote, "and speaking as a philosopher, since the soul is not found without body and yet is not body, it may be in one body or in another, and pass from body to body." Such outrageous thinking was not to be tolerated by the Inquisition. For daring to vent his original mind, Bruno was imprisoned by the Venetian authorities for seven years and eventually burned at the stake in Rome in 1600.

Twentieth-century intellectual freedom was on the side of Rudolf Steiner, the founder of Anthroposophy, when he chose to augment the teachings of the cyclic school. Comparing the human life cycle with that of the planets, he wrote: "Just as the human being passes from incarnation to incarnation, passes through repeated Earth lives, so did our Earth pass through other states before it came into the state in which it is today. There are earlier incarnations of a planet just as there are earlier incarnations of a human being. Everything in the great world and in the little world is subject to the law of reincarnation."

Testimony both ancient and modern proclaims the same message. Death and renewal are one. Mind and matter are one. We are the same everlasting energy that assumes a multitude of forms in order to interact with itself unto infinity. In the materialization of this energy, patterns of recurrence manifest themselves in planetary positioning, the seasons, weather systems, tides, organic metamorphoses and the fortunes of the human, animal and vegetable kingdoms. Night yields to day; calm gives way to storm; rainwater evaporates to become rain once more. From the ruins of empire are born new civilizations.

Some aboriginal tribes, still cherishing the innate belief of their ancestors, ally themselves with this cosmic procedure by seeing the monthly "death" and "birth" of the moon as a guarantee of their reincarnation. In so doing they are expressing a feeling of integration, of unity, with their farthest surroundings. How ironic it is that the technology which has tended to alienate modern society from the natural rhythms conducive to such experience should be used by the "new physics" to rediscover—intellectually, at least—this Oneness, this ordinary miracle of perpetual rebirth.

4

Prodigies, Plato
and Precognition

*The endless legacy of the past to the present is the
secret source of human genius.*

HONORÉ DE BALZAC

*Forgetfulness of the past may be one of the condi-
tions of an entrance upon a new stage of existence.
The body, which is the organ of sense-perception,
may be quite as much a hindrance as a help to
remembrance. In that case, casual gleams of memory, giving us sudden, abrupt and momentary revelations of the past, are precisely the phenomena we
would expect to meet with.*

WILLIAM KNIGHT

On a hot day in August, 1971, author Frank De Felitta
and his wife, Dorothy, were relaxing beside the swimming
pool at their $200,000 Los Angeles home when they suddenly
heard brilliant ragtime piano playing coming from the house.
Rushing inside, they were amazed to find their six-year-old
son, Raymond, dexterously running his hands up and down

their piano keyboard which he had never before attempted to play. "Daddy, my fingers are doing it by themselves!" exclaimed Raymond. "Isn't it wonderful?"

At first, his parents weren't so sure. While Dorothy screamed: "What the hell's he doing?" and refused to go near her son, Frank was overtaken by an unaccountable surge of anger. "The impact would not have been greater had we found him floating around the room," he recalled. Raymond went on to be recognized throughout the United States for his accomplished playing which veers toward the strident jazz style of Fats Waller who died in 1945. And Frank De Felitta became "a grudging and cynical convert" to reincarnation—the only logical explanation for what he had seen and heard. His son's behavior, he said, "was not consistent with anything we had been given to understand. It was beyond my comprehension. From never even experimenting with the piano as some young children do, here was my tiny son playing like a professional for up to five hours a day." The experience moved Frank to write the reincarnational novel *Audrey Rose* which has since been made into a popular film.

Flabbergasting though it must have been, Raymond's impromptu performance was no more than a modern manifestation of an infrequent yet ancient phenomenon, the very existence of which implies that past-life talents can be responsible for innate ability. As long ago as the first century before Christ, Cicero, the Roman orator, statesman and philosopher, maintained that the speed with which children grasp innumerable facts is "a strong proof of men knowing most things before birth." But the foundations, at least for the modern world, of the teaching that all knowledge is recollection were laid by Socrates and Plato some three hundred and fifty years earlier. "Knowledge easily acquired," stated Plato's Theory of Reminiscence, "is that which the enduring self had in an earlier life, so that it flows back easily." Which is to say that genius is the flowering of past-life experience. So imbued was the old world with this way of thinking that the word "education" originally meant "to draw from that which already was known." Centuries later, the French philosopher René Descartes played a variation on this hoary theme when he remarked that human beings seem to possess an anterior memory that shows itself in differing intuitions, predispositions, talents, insights and inspirations, all suggesting the promptings of earlier rehearsals.

When William Wordsworth wrote that "birth is but a sleep and a forgetting" he probably wasn't aware of the world's wonder children with their rare talent for awakening and remembering. Nevertheless, child prodigies and youngsters like Raymond De Felitta, who are seemingly gripped by flashes of their past, bear out the poet's words, and provide strong circumstantial evidence to show that what may be consciously forgotten is not necessarily lost. No Western child prodigy has been known to remember a past life, but reincarnation appears to offer the best explanation for:

Christian Friedrich Heinecken. Known as the "Infant of Lubeck," he is said to have talked within a few hours of his birth in 1721. At one, he knew the main events related in the first five books of the Old Testament; at two, the whole of Biblical history; and at three, he understood the outlines of world history and geography, while speaking Latin and French as well as his native German. Intrigued by the boy's reputation, the King of Denmark had him brought to Copenhagen in 1724. Shortly after this, however, the Infant of Lubeck fell ill and predicted his own death within the year. He died at the tender age of four.

Wolfgang Amadeus Mozart. At four years of age this world-famous composer of the eighteenth century wrote minuets, a piano concerto and a sonata. His compositions at this age were not only technically accurate but also extremely difficult. At seven, he composed a full-length opera.

Jean Louis Cardiac. Born in 1719, this French wonder child was able to repeat the alphabet when just three months old. At three years, he could read Latin, and at four, he could translate the language into either French or English. He died in Paris at the age of seven.

Miguel Mantilla. An article in a 1928 edition of the *British Journal of Psychical Research* featured the calendar wizardry of this two-year-old Mexican tot. Within fifteen seconds, Miguel could answer such questions as: "In what years will February 4 be a Friday?" and "What date was the second Sunday in 1840?"

"Blind Tom" Wiggins. The sightless child of a Negro slave

living in Georgia, Tom played the piano like a consummate professional at four years of age. His master hired a music teacher to encourage the boy's amazing talent. But after hearing Tom play, the teacher refused the appointment, declaring: "That boy already knows more about music than I will ever know." Tom went on to give concerts both in America and abroad. Yet, away from the piano, he remained a near-idiot with a vocabulary of no more than a few hundred words. He died, world-famous, in 1908.

John Stuart Mill. The English philosopher-economist who lived from 1806 to 1873 knew Greek at three years of age and, at six, could read Xenophon, Herodotus, Aesop and Lucian.

José Capablanca. A Cuban prodigy who, by the age of four, was already a brilliant chess player. He seldom lost a game even when playing against experts who had spent years perfecting their moves. He went on to become world champion and died in 1942.

Giannella de Marco. On March 12, 1953, Giannella, an eight-year-old Italian girl, conducted the London Philharmonic Orchestra at the Royal Albert Hall, London, in works by Weber, Haydn, Wagner and Beethoven. A review in *The Times* said: "She plies a clear, generous beat and plainly has the music at her finger-ends. . . . There is an unnerving maturity in her intellectual accomplishment. . . ." The London concert appearance was the one-hundred twenty-third of her career, which began at the age of four.

Carl Friedrich Gauss. When not quite three years of age, the boy who went on to become the greatest mathematician of the nineteenth century is said to have mentally followed a calculation of his father's and spotted a mistake. The calculation was related to the wages of some of his father's employees.

Medical experts have attempted to explain child wonders by pointing to glandular abnormalities that cause certain parts of the nervous system to reach peak activity in advance of other bodily areas. That most prodigies are male and infantile gland disorders are mainly found in boys, tends to support this view. Yet the phenomena can only be partially explained by a purely physical interpretation. It's worth noting that Edgar Cayce and other clairvoyant investigators are in agreement that the glands are the primary agents of karma, the impersonal and ongoing thrust of cause and effect integral to the doctrine of rebirth.

Chang and Eng

The most popular argument against reincarnation as the source of precocious talent is the theory that memory is transferred genetically from generation to generation through what have been dubbed the psychogenes. It is contested that prodigies somehow dip into this genetic material, this anterior thread of DNA molecules, in order to draw on a skill well developed in an ancestor. But if heredity can explain similarities among family members—and there's no denying the hand-me-down pattern of physical resemblance—it cannot pretend to account for the differences. One would think that conjoined or "Siamese" twins, having uniform genetic material and a uniform early environment, would develop similarly as human beings. Not so. Chang and Eng, the pair of conjoined twins whose nationality inspired the term "Siamese twins," developed demonstrably different personalities. Chang, for example, loved drinking liquor and sank into periodic alcoholic debauches while Eng was a teetotaller. Chang and Eng are not alone in their variance. ". . . Siamese twins are almost without exception more different in various ways than any but a very few pairs of separate one-egg twins," wrote H. H. Newman in *Multiple Human Births*. "One of the most difficult problems faced by the twinning specialist is that of accounting for this unexpected dissimilarity of the components of Siamese twin pairs." Such glaring disparities, which are also reflected in identical twins, quadruplets and quintuplets, continue to plague geneticists, most of whom are loath to consider the possible explanation of divergent past-life experience.

Recent studies showing the ability of tiny babies to mimic adults within hours of their birth appear to underline the Platonic assertion that all learning is remembering. Research from the University of Miami Medical School reported in the *Brain Mind Bulletin* of November 22, 1982, detected the "remarkable ability" of infants averaging thirty-six hours old to imitate happy, sad and surprised expressions modeled by adults. "Because of their early appearance and apparent universality, these basic facial expressions may reflect innate processes," the study concluded. Dr. Tom Verny, a Toronto psychiatrist not given to metaphysical speculation, tells in *The Secret Life of the Unborn Child* how the animated faces of researchers in Seattle, Washington, were imitated by a nursery full of babies—some of whom were only one hour old! "When a researcher stuck out his or her tongue, made a face, or wiggled fingers in front of a baby, the child often responded in kind," writes Verny. "This (and other experiments like it) demonstrates conclusively the presence of well-developed (one could say adult) thinking, including the handling of abstract ideas in the new-born."

Naturally, the question that shrieks for reply is: Where does such behavior come from? Dr. Verny is not a reincarnationist, but he does allow that reincarnation could provide the answer. He revealed that certain case material gathered for his book, material which demonstrates how the thoughts and feelings of pregnant mothers affect their unborn children, "could not be explained in terms of physiological and behavioral communications." His studies and clinical experience suggest that, besides the memory of the central nervous system which becomes functional between the fifth and sixth months of pregnancy, there is another memory system which cannot be accounted for. Nevertheless, being pragmatically scientific in his approach, Verny is uncomfortable with rebirth as an explanation, preferring to believe such recollection is cellular, coded in the DNA molecules. While he has had "inklings of something mystical and spiritual while working with my patients," Verny admits to being "doubly careful that I'm not reduced to accepting a world of fantasy, make-believe or wish fulfillment." Yet even this self-imposed safeguard cannot invalidate the experiences of several of Verny's patients who have slipped unbidden into "past lives" when lulled with music and hypnotic suggestion for exploration of the prenatal state. One patient, fifty-year-old John Kerr, reported being aware of his parents' contrasting emotions at the moment of his conception. Another, commercial artist Denise Maxwell, thirty-three, vividly experienced three past-life deaths in the course of an hour: first, as a young woman in a Central

American tribe, then as a primitive Scandinavian hunter buried in the sitting position with his knife and spear, and finally, as a poverty-stricken male artist in eighteenth-century Europe.

While the thrust of Verny's research demonstrates how maternal emotions can profoundly affect the child in the womb, Dr. Ian Stevenson has shown, as an offshoot of his child studies suggestive of reincarnation, that the fetus can provoke reactions in the mother by making her conform to its tastes of the previous lifetime. In a number of cases studied intensively by Stevenson, the mother of a child subject reported that, during pregnancy, she had been seized by an unusual craving for a food relished by the previous personality subsequently claimed by her child. In other cases, the mother had experienced revulsion for a food which also happened to fall foul of the tastebuds of the claimed previous personality.

In one case from Sri Lanka, the mother of Gamini Jayasena experienced a marked aversion for meat during her pregnancy in 1962—an aversion not encountered while carrying her three other children. Gamini later claimed to have lived as Palitha Senewiratne who had died at eight years of age on July 28, 1960. Palitha had given up eating meat at five years of age and, after making this decision, had vomited while reluctantly trying to comply with a family request to go back to his meat-eating ways.

In another Sri Lanka case, the mother of Sujuth Lakmal Jayaratne suddenly developed, in the course of her pregnancy, a fascination for wade—a hot spiced food made of dhal, chilies and coconut oil—and manioc, a type of yam. It so happened that Sujuth, who was born on August 7, 1969, remembered the life of Sammy Fernando who had been struck and killed by a truck roughly six months earlier. Fernando had been particularly fond of the food Sujuth's mother craved.

Heredity can only explain so much about human succession and the range of predispositions which we suppress or develop in the course of a lifetime. Thomas Henry Huxley, one of the most outstanding scientists of the nineteenth century, was convinced that "every one of us bears upon him obvious marks of his parentage, perhaps of remoter relationships." But he didn't rule out the possibility of rebirth working in tandem with this hereditary influence. In his essay *Evolution and Ethics,* written in 1897, Huxley argued that "none but very hasty thinkers" will reject reincarnation on the grounds of inherent absurdity.

The Russian writer and lecturer P. D. Ouspensky found the "various ingenious theories" of heredity, hidden instincts and unconscious memory all acceptable, but he also found that they left very much unexplained. "Until we find it possible to recognize that we have lived before," he declared, "very much will remain in us that we shall never be able to understand."

According to the insights of those who have taken LSD under experimental conditions, the laws of reincarnation operate independently of the subject's biological lineage and the genetic transfer of idioplasma. "The assignment of an individual spiritual entity to a particular physical body and a specific life seems to bypass biological hereditary lines and violate genetic laws," Czechoslovakian-born psychotherapist Dr. Stanislav Grof has noted:

Electing for Birth

A 1978 research study in which 750 subjects were hypnotized and guided back to a state just before birth satisfied clinical psychologist Dr. Helen Wambach that heredity and reincarnation operate independently but complement each other. She found that the individual entity opts for materialization in a specific body in a particular hereditary line. Eighty-one per cent of Dr. Wambach's subjects said they chose to be born, most choosing reluctantly after consultation with spiritual advisers. Although 90 per cent of the group spoke of death as being pleasant, only 26 per cent looked forward to the coming lifetime. Noted one participant: "My feelings about the prospect of coming into the current lifetime were, 'Well, guess I'll go get stripped down some more.'" (Case A–418) Another said: ". . . It was something that had to be done, like washing the floor when it's dirty." (Case A–285)

Eighty-seven per cent reported knowing parents, lovers, relatives and friends of the current lifetime in varied relationships both in past lives and in the state between lives. "Blood may be thicker than water," writes Dr. Wambach in her book *Life Before Life*, "but judging by my results, past-life ties are a lot thicker than blood." As farfetched as the idea of group reincarnation might seem to some people, the meeting of cells in all the right places within the human body is surely no more miraculous a proposition. Time and time again, Dr. Wambach's subjects emerged from their trance to relay the same story—that we come back with the same souls to share a variety of relationships not only with those we love but also with those who inspire fear and hatred. Such statements can only lead to further conjecture: perhaps the individual must know *from personal experience* life's every vicissitude; perhaps spiritual evolution demands our rotational embodiment so that we may truly understand the host of conflicting human perspectives. Perhaps we can learn and grow only by being rich and poor, beautiful and ugly, healthy and disease-ridden, master and slave, murderer and murderer's victim. . . .

Research undertaken by the world's leading expert on death and dying, Swiss-born psychiatrist Dr. Elisabeth Kübler-Ross, lends credence to the suggestion that there is an evolutionary requirement to plunge repeatedly into the brackish water of earthly existence. Dr. Ross writes from her Shanti Nilaya foundation in Escondido, California, that the purpose of life on the physical plane is "to learn and grow and to participate in the spiritual evolution of man. In order to fulfill our destiny we have to learn certain lessons and pass certain tests. And we can regard death as a graduation from the physical plane only when we have learned all these lessons and passed those tests. In our present society, where negativity is so overwhelming and evident in every area from raising children to the killing of our fellow humans in war, in violence and crime, it is practically impossible to fulfill our destiny in one lifetime. When we have not learned our lessons or if we have broken some universal law like 'Thou shalt not kill' we have a chance to return into a physical body of another human being. . . . We then choose our own parents, our place of birth and an environment that will make it most likely to learn the lessons that ought to be learned. . . ."

Dr. Richard Alpert, an American social scientist and spiritual teacher who often goes under the name of Ram

Dass, expressed his perception of the guiding role of the subconscious in selecting lives of appropriate experience when he wrote that, before birth, people "know just what they're buying into. They say, 'I'm buying into these parents, this experience. I'm going to be in this life, I'm going to have one eye, I'm going to be a cripple, I'm going to end up being beaten to death on the street in Benares and that's what I need. O.K., here I go.' You dive down in, and the veil is lowered. There you are, and here we are, and we run through this one, and then we get all finished and we come back out of it and we wake up. O.K., you ran that one off; now let's see what's next. What I need to be now is a duke, and I might have to wait thousands of years for that one."

Reincarnationists like to speak of the Earth plane as a training school to which we, the pupils, return lifeterm after lifeterm, each of us bearing our own spiritual satchel of inclinations, wisdom and experience garnered from previous existences. So many are the past glories and graduations, trials and reversals, that to remember them all in each successive life could overwhelm to the point of inertia—just as knowing the fortunes of the future could sap all desire for living. "It is nature's kindness that we do not remember past births," remarked Mohandas K. Gandhi, the great Indian philosopher and apostle of non-violence. "Life would be a burden if we carried such a tremendous load of memories."

Yet it is possible, even therapeutically helpful, to reach into the fathomless past to retrieve some of this obscured recollection. Knowing and accepting crucial events of the past can transform present experience, as the next chapter will show.

5

Healing the Scars
of Centuries

*There is no disease known to man the cause of
which is entirely determined in what is called his
own lifetime.*

ARTHUR GUIRDHAM

*Past lives therapy allows you to stop doing things to
people because you have to and to start doing things
with people because you want to.*

MORRIS NETHERTON

The clinical validity of past-life therapy has been established beyond doubt. With increasing regularity over the last
thirty years, hundreds of thousands of suffering people have
been lulled into altered states of consciousness and guided
through the veil of time to re-live, or view with detached
wonderment, critical episodes of former existences. What
they experience is another, superimposed reality fraught with
all the immediacy of the therapist's couch—it might be a
workhouse in nineteenth-century England, a mud hut in
ancient Somalia or a Mayan temple courtyard deep in the
Central American jungle.

To match the onrushing change of scene, the clients of past-life therapy find that they assume appropriate identities from out of the amnesia of hundreds, even thousands, of years. Anything can—and does—happen. A hearty-voiced plumber might become a lisping peasant girl; a placid secretary could take on the persona of a fierce warrior. Some people observe their transformation as if they were seated in the front row of a theatre of the mind; others enter the very body of the character. And then there are those who sense or feel events unfolding from afar. However a past life is perceived, the aim of the therapy is to mine the experience of the soul; to heal through self-understanding.

Having ensured that the source of a patient's troublesome condition cannot be detected in the current lifetime, the therapist knows the canker is lurking somewhere in the individual's repertoire of past lives. This buried trauma invariably reverberates in the life of today as physiological pain or mental anguish, or both. For past-life therapy confirms that mind and body share the closest of relationships, that a psychological component exists for every physical disease, and vice versa. While many hours spent probing successive lives may be required to locate the source of the aggravation, healing is often rapid and dramatic once the pertinent information has been wrested from the subconscious. No one can state with certainty how this remedial effect is wrought, but it would appear that the very act of confronting and accepting negativity long trapped in the psyche provokes some alchemy of liberation. The release of blocked energy seems to encourage the evaporation of the cause of the ailment which could be cancer, multiple sclerosis, ulcers, arthritis, obesity, stuttering, migraine headaches, depression, learning disability, epilepsy, every conceivable form of phobia, addiction, allergies, sexual inadequacy—the lot! The end of the regression isn't necessarily the end of the experience. Confused memories, emotions and expanded awareness of the trauma can invade the patient's dreams and waking consciousness for weeks or even months afterwards.

So past-life therapy often works where conventional treatment fails, but does that mean reincarnation is repsonsible for the plethora of "past lives?" Not necessarily. Telepathy, the uncharted ocean of the collective unconscious, spirit possession, ancestral memory, intricate sub-personalities created by the ever-inventive mind and pure fantasy are some alternative explanations. Yet the rebirth hypothesis, being the most straightforward interpretation, keeps bobbing up like an apple in a bucket of water. Patients' oft-expressed strong identification with the personalities assumed under hypnosis as well as the fact that many a past-life individual has been historically verified, strengthens the case for reincarnation. So does the research of Dr. Helen Wambach whose subjects, regardless of their sex in the current lifetime, have divided strictly according to biological fact by recalling 50.6 per cent male and 49.4 per cent female lives when regressed to time periods as far back as 2000 B.C. The studies of Dr. Wambach—even though her subjects were primarily white, middle-class Americans—also accurately reflect race, class and population distribution in the real historical world as well as the clothing and footwear worn across the centuries and the type of food eaten and utensils used.

Nevertheless, proof of reincarnation is no more accessible to past-life therapists than it is to investigators of infant recall. "Even if every detail given by a patient under hypnosis is shown to be an accurate statement about a person who had once lived," says hypnotherapist Dr. Edith Fiore, "you are not proving the patient actually lived the life. You are just showing that someone lived and died. The patient could be tapping into someone else's thought forms." Which isn't to say that Dr. Fiore, a clinical psychologist from Saratoga, California, discounts reincarnation. Far from it. In eight years of using hypnosis as the mainstay of her practice, she has swung from disbelief to a 99 per cent conviction in rebirth. "If someone's phobia is eliminated instantly and permanently by the remembrance of an event from the past, it seems to make logical sense that that event must have happened," she declares.

Certainly, this viewpoint is disputed by hypnotherapists who don't believe in reincarnation. Such a man is Dr. Gerald Edelstein, a staff psychiatrist at Herrick Memorial Hospital in Berkeley, California, who has found that, despite his ideological prejudice, several of his patients have slipped into past lives—with terrific results! He admits candidly: "These experiences, for reasons I cannot explain, almost always lead to rapid improvements in the patients' lives."

Says Dr. Morris Netherton, a pioneering Los Angeles practitioner: "Many people go away believing in reincarnation as a result of their experience; others see it as symbolic, metaphorical. But what is the logical answer? That it actually happened! It took nature ten million years to build the Grand Canyon and that's just a big hole in the ground. I can't believe it takes just seventy or eighty years to build a man's soul."

What Netherton does believe is that "everything in the mind comes from what has gone on before." He defines imagination as "the sum total of everything that ever happened to you in every lifetime you ever lived." It's a grand vision, created and corroborated by the testimony of more than eight thousand patients. This chubby, energetic personality whose coffee mug bears the slogan "World's Greatest Doctor" was raised a fundamental southern Methodist. He hardly considered the idea of reincarnation until seventeen years ago when, beset by unemployment, a chronic bleeding ulcer and feelings of emotional inadequacy, he turned in despair to conventional therapy. "In the third session I talked about the pain I was feeling," he said, "and the next thing I knew I was in a different place." Suddenly, spontaneously, Netherton visualized himself in a Mexican institution for the criminally insane. The year was 1818. A guard had kicked him in the stomach in the exact spot where his ulcer had flared. He understood that his lands had been seized by his wife and her family who had conspired to have him committed. At the same time, he was intuitively aware that his wife in that life was also Carol, the woman he is married to today. (Being told of this later at a local restaurant, Carol "passed out in her mashed potatoes," to quote her husband.)

Whatever the truth of this flashback of confrontation, Netherton was at once granted "amazing relief" from pain that has never returned. Hired as a probation officer, he went on to win a master's degree in counseling and a doctorate in psychology. Yet he was not converted instantly to a belief in reincarnation. Conversion came slowly as a by-product of his self-development as a therapist in which he personally underwent more than 1,200 hours of past-life examination. The

Netherton Method, expounded in the best-seller *Past Lives Therapy* and since practised not only in Los Angeles but also in training offices in Montreal, São Paulo, Brazil and Stuttgart, West Germany, is unique in that it relies, at the outset, on a patient's use of specific recurring or out-of-place phrases. Guided by these key phrases, for example, "It's hopeless" or "They're holding me down," Netherton attempts to unlock the unconscious by asking the patient to concentrate on repeating them. This repetition jogs the patient's mind to an image, the starting point for a detailed reconstruction of pain, guilt and trauma. Netherton says his patients *must* relive traumatic experiences of the past in order to clear up their current problems. "You have to bring it into the body," he declares. "That's the only way you can be assured you're getting accurate information." And so, often screaming, writhing, moaning, weeping and breaking into foreign languages, Netherton's subjects enter their battened-down ugliness in order to leave it all behind. Past births and deaths—common sources of behavioral disorder—are commonly re-enacted. And Netherton insists that no past-life trauma is completely erased without detecting the unresolved prenatal incident, or incidents, that activate a track of problematical past lives in the individual. Noting that the fetus is extremely sensitive to the mother's thoughts and feelings (an observation substantiated by the findings of Dr. Tom Verny), Netherton writes in *Past Lives Therapy*:

> The unborn child, awaiting the beginning of conscious life, is profoundly affected by this prenatal awareness. With no conscious mind to discern or interpret, the unconscious plays back any past-life incidents triggered by events in the mother's life. These incidents shape the behavior patterns of the child. At birth the infant will begin a life of trying to resolve those past-life events without ever knowing what they are.

It matters not whether Netherton's patients, who range from priests to physicists, believe in reincarnation: the recall flows just the same, restricted neither by creed nor color. Whites, for example, hark back to existences as Negro slaves;

Chicanos remember fighting as British soldiers in World War II, and as if to invalidate the genetic memory interpretation, many have described being alive during their parents' lifetimes! "Some patients start by feeling that they are 'making up' parts of what they tell me," Netherton has written, "but they soon discover that they cannot change the content of their past-life incidents, and must reveal the most personal and painful aspects of the stories they had thought were imaginary. This is what most quickly convinces the skeptic. He begins by saying the first thing that comes into his head simply to placate me. But the moment he comes face to face with his pain, he can no longer deny the validity of the therapy."

Among the conclusions Netherton has gleaned from his patients' testimony is that each individual returns to Earth at the identical stage of development reached at the time of death. He urges people, wherever possible, not to enlist artificial support at death "unless you want to come back in that way, being supported. You come back as you went out. It's a continuous journey." Abortion, according to Netherton's findings, is "the killing of something that has feeling." Time and again, he has asked patients who have regressed to aborted embryos whether they have a message for their mothers and often that message is a haunting "I'll be back." The act of abortion appears to set up a pattern of incompletion for the protagonists which can exert a domino effect from life to life. In fact, the recurrence of similar patterns and problems over a sequence of lives is a common phenomenon perceived by Netherton as the unconscious mind's way of resolving specific issues through repeated trials of close resemblance.

Victims of the Self

Dr. Edith Fiore singles out guilt as the architect of the most profoundly negative effects in her patients' experiences. "When I see someone with four or five symptoms, when they are losing in the game of life, it's as if they are saying: 'I don't deserve this, that and the other,'" says the author of *You Have Been Here Before*. She also finds that "nobody is ever a victim without a cause": her patients have always earned their discomfort by their own actions.

Illustrating this system of cause and effect, which mirrors the Hindu and Buddhist doctrine of karma, is one of Fiore's most dramatic cases. A woman in her mid-thirties, who booked therapy in desperation after undergoing twelve operations for bone cancer, saw herself, under hypnosis, as a priestess in an ancient cult which practised human sacrifice. Her role was to drink the blood of the sacrificial victims, a chore she detested. But, as the choice was drink, or be sacrificed yourself, she hardened herself to the task. After the regression, the woman submitted to a blood test prior to yet another expected operation. The test revealed there were no longer any living cancer cells in her body and the operation was canceled. Now that several years have elapsed and the woman appears to be completely healed, it's interesting to reflect that blood is manufactured in the bone marrow—the very site of her affliction.

Speaking to the second annual conference of the Association for Past Life Research and Therapy in Los Angeles in October, 1982, Fiore declared: "Other therapies address the symptoms and leave the cause untouched. Past-life therapy attacks the root cause. There isn't a single physical problem that can't be resolved by good past-life treatment." This statement was the product of her clinical experience which has shown that all sorts of ailments can be traced back to past lives. She has found that practically all patients who are overweight by more than ten pounds have had a lifetime in which they starved to death or suffered food deprivation for long periods. Irrational fears of snakes, of fire, of being alone, of flying, of darkness, of crowds, of natural cataclysms such as earthquakes and storms, have been relieved by coming to terms with terrifying past-life misfortunes. One teenage boy, for example, was troubled by only being able to fall asleep if he was alone and in total silence. His difficulty was traced to his having been bayoneted to death by a Japanese soldier while sleeping on the beach of a Pacific island during the Second World War. The origins of migraine headaches have been variously determined as clubbing, guillotining, shooting, stoning, hanging or scalping in another existence. Those with chronic abdominal pains have re-lived having their bellies run through with swords, bayonets or knives. Even menstrual problems have been seen to stem from past-life sexual trauma, while instant attractions, dislikes and feelings of familiarity or distrust have become perfectly understandable after a glimpse of events in former existences.

"Are they putting on an act?" Fiore asks rhetorically of her patients in *You Have Been Here Before*. "If so, most should be nominated for Academy Awards. I have listened to and watched people in past-life regressions under hypnosis for thousands of hours. I am convinced there is no deliberate, nor conscious, attempt to deceive. The tears, shaking, flinching, smiling, gasping for breath, groaning, sweating and other physical manifestations are all too real."

It's fitting that Californians, with their legendary affluence and fixation for self-discovery, should be the world's greatest patrons of past-life therapy, which can cost as much as $300 an hour in the redwood state. Yet the origins of hypnotic regression—which gripped California in the mid-seventies and has failed to let go—can be traced to turn-of-the-century France and the experiments of the enigmatic Colonel Albert de Rochas. Conducting transverse and longitudinal passes with his hands in the style of Franz Anton Mesmer, the Austrian physician who gave his name to hypnosis or "mesmerism," Rochas swept his subjects back into a succession of past lives.

One of these subjects was eighteen-year-old Mlle. Marie Mayo, an engineer's daughter, who was first taken back to the age of eight when, having attended a school in Beirut, she wrote her name in Arabic. Beyond her birth, she called herself Lina, the daughter of a fisherman in Brittany. She related how she married, at twenty, a fisherman called Yvon, how her only child died at the age of two, and how, in a fit of despair after her husband's death in a shipwreck, she threw herself into the sea from the top of a precipice. Marie Mayo re-lived the convulsions of drowning before passing into another incarnation, this time as a man—Charles Mauville, a clerk and murderer who lived during the time of Louis XVI. Still further back, she became Madeleine de Saint-Marc, whose husband was a gentleman of the French court.

As fascinating and as plausible as most of Rochas' subjects were, they never gave precise information which could be checked out with historical fact even though the places and families mentioned were often known to have existed. This frustration caused Rochas—who tried in vain to divert his subjects' recall so as to counteract any suggestion that he was prompting telepathically the experimental evidence—to reflect upon "the darkness in which all observers have to struggle at the beginning of every new science."

For years, psychiatrists and psychologists interpreted their patients' occasional spontaneous recall from other lives as mental derangement. But there were always investigators knocking at the door of the unknown. Sweden's John Björkhem (1910-1963) advanced the fledgling science by conducting hundreds of regression experiments in which the previous lives claimed under hypnosis were frequently verified. And in 1950, Dr. Alexander Cannon, an Englishman awarded degrees by nine European universities, grudgingly gave in to the evidence of rebirth produced by 1,382 volunteers who, when regressed, spoke of living in various time periods as far back as several thousand years before Christ. He wrote in *The Power Within*:

> For years the theory of reincarnation was a night-mare to me and I did my best to disprove it and even argued with my trance subjects to the effect that they were talking nonsense. Yet as the years went by one subject after another told me the same story in spite of different and varied conscious be-liefs. Now well over a thousand cases have been so investigated and I have to admit that there is such a thing as reincarnation.

Cannon specialized in discovering hidden complexes and fears engendered by traumatic incidents in past lives. Holding that the work of the great psychoanalyst Sigmund Freud had been "outflanked" by reincarnation, he declared: "The majority of people do not benefit from psychoanalysis because the trauma lies not in this life but in a past life."

Similar conclusions were reached independently by English psychiatrist Dr. Arthur Guirdham through what he calls "a purely intellectual process." Verifying and cross-referencing over many years a torrent of obscure suggestions, medical symptoms, psychic revelations, automatic writing and recurring dreams, Guirdham came to believe that he is one of a group of people who have reincarnated together in five separate time periods. Having completed forty-four years of medical practice and written fourteen books, Guirdham, now seventy-eight, maintains he has remained a skeptic ever since being nicknamed "Doubting Thomas" as a boy. But he declares quite emphatically: "If I didn't believe in reincarnation on the evidence I'd received I'd be mentally defective." The evidence—vast in quantity and complex in nature—does not involve hypnotic regression, but it does point to disease originating in past incarnations. Guirdham cites many examples of the "anniversary phenomenon" in which illness or depression is suffered on days coinciding with tragic happenings in previous incarnations. He argues that while the short duration of symptoms often corresponds to brief incidents in previous lives, longer disturbances such as full-blown disease will have a more lasting counterpart in a previous existence.

The case of Bonnie Brown, a Toronto fashion model who was regressed to a sickly past life in a concentration camp, backs up this viewpoint. At twenty-nine years of age, Bonnie had been plagued with repeated attacks of bronchitis every winter since childhood. Induced into an altered state of consciousness by hypnotherapist Beverly Janus, she encountered five different lifetimes in the space of an hour. Then she found herself as a young woman in a small East European town wearing drab clothes and a headscarf. With her neighbors, she was taken from her earthen-floored hut and led to a train by soldiers wearing Second World War uniforms. There was no food or water on the train and she was cold and racked with coughing. (Bonnie coughed throughout the regression and felt so cold she had to be wrapped in blankets.) After several days' journey, Bonnie and her fellow captives were herded into a camp fenced with barbed wire. "I was standing at the fence with my hands on the wire," Bonnie recalls. "I was coughing blood. I remember thinking: 'I don't want to live any more.' No one seemed to care. I was coughing and coughing until the end." It was then that Beverly Janus instructed her hypnotized patient that she would no longer be affected by the bad effects of the past. Since that regression in 1972, when she confronted her sickness in what appeared to be her previous incarnation, Bonnie hasn't experienced a trace of bronchial trouble. She says: "I feel that reincarnation is the best explanation for what happened. But if it was only an exploration of my psyche to show me that I no longer need to have bronchitis, who cares? The main thing is that it works."

Twenty-seven-year-old Shirley Kleppe-Moran, a research subject of Dr. Helen Wambach, was similarly relieved of periodic seizures for which there was no medical explanation or salvation. The seizures, lasting from fifteen minutes to an hour, made her body "feel like it was going a million miles an hour" and had afflicted her since the age of seven. Under hypnosis, she entered the life of a young French girl living on the coast of Normandy in the sixteenth century. Suspected of being a witch because she was seen visiting a sick boy who had subsequently died, she was chased by torch-carrying villagers to a line of cliffs where she jumped to her death. Shirley relived her leap into mid-air as the intense, emotional equivalent of her seizures which, since that day in 1977, have never returned.

By no means confined to the seekers and self-analysts of the West, past-life therapy is earnestly pursued behind the Iron Curtain. Moscow specialist Varvara Ivanova, held in high esteem by Soviet scientists and writers, has found that regression allows people not only to perceive the reasons for their sufferings and the educational goal of their "chain of life," but also to understand their habits, idiosyncracies and unconscious gestures. In a statement that could have come from the lips of Morris Netherton or a hundred other Western therapists, she avers that similar difficulties will crop up in successive lifetimes "until one learns to fight adversity. You have to solve them. If you don't solve them in this lifetime, they appear again and again in different forms and situations in the same life, and in other ones, till you learn to master them in the right way."

Bridey Hysteria

Not all regression has a therapeutic objective. Which is just as well because past-life therapists, with healing as their aim, care little for shouldering the burden of dissecting the mystery behind the daily miracle. Usually, regressionists interested in the phenomena for its own sake are the ones who scrutinize their labors for any leads which might provide detailed evidence for rebirth. Certainly, the sole objective of part-time hypnotist Morey Bernstein in 1952 was to test his ability to probe memories before birth—a phenomenon he had only read about. Imagine his excitement when his subject, Colorado housewife Virginia Tighe (a name to be quickly submerged by the alias Ruth Simmons) slipped into what was to become her celebrated Bridey Murphy persona from nineteenth-century Ireland. Bridey took the world by storm when the story of Bernstein's regressions were splashed across newspapers and magazines. "Come As You Were" costume parties were held, Reincarnation Cocktails were mixed in bars, songs about rebirth crowded the airwaves and Paramount Pictures produced a Bridey Murphy movie. *The Search For Bridey Murphy*, Bernstein's account of his adventures in hypnotism by candle flame, went on to become a million copy best-seller. On at least one occasion the past-life fever got out of hand. A teenager in Shawnee, Oklahoma, was so carried away by the mass enthusiasm that he shot himself, leaving a note saying that he intended to conduct his own investigation of reincarnation.

Although the landmarks of Bridey's existence (born in County Cork, 1798, the daughter of Duncan and Kathleen Murphy, she married Brian MacCarthy and died childless in Belfast at the age of sixty-six after falling down some steps) were clearly stated in Irish brogue, the dates of her birth, marriage and death were impossible to confirm because no records were kept in Ireland before 1864. Nevertheless, the stores mentioned by Bridey—Caden House, Farr's and John Carrigan's—were found to have existed. A host of obsolete Irish words, among them "flats" for platters and "slip" for a child's pinafore or frock, had been used accurately. Local events and details of household furniture, domestic articles, food, kitchen utensils, coinage, books, popular songs and dances, farming practices and the street lighting of Belfast— "poles with lights on them"—were all graphically described. She even related the correct procedure for kissing the Blarney stone and, being particularly fond of dancing, rounded off one hypnotic session by performing *The Morning Jig* complete with its finale of a stylized yawn. At her funeral, Bridey was aware of the playing of the Uilleann pipes—a popular instrument of the day owing to its soft tone.

More than anything, it is the accumulation of minor verifications that gives the case its core of credibility. For a while, skeptics made great play of Bridey's childhood reference to a metal bed because such beds were thought to have been unknown in Ireland before 1850. Further inquiry, however, showed that metal beds were advertized as early as 1802. "Research," wrote journalist William J. Barker, who traveled to Ireland to prepare a 19,000-word report entitled *The Truth About Bridey Murphy*, "is Bridey's best ally."

Since the Bridey Murphy sensation, regressionists around the world have been eager to emulate the feat with distinctive cases of their own. From the Cheshire home of Joe Keeton, Britain's busiest regressionist, to the corporate office in Malibu, California, of Dick Sutphen, a man who markets reincarnation like soapsuds, the tapes and casebooks of rebirth are swollen with evidence for all who are willing to be persuaded.

There are few cases more convincing than teacher Margaret Baker's remarkable recall of the life and death of gypsy horse dealer Tyzo Boswell. In 1978, during a taped regression in which she was suspicious of her *gorgio* or non-gypsy interviewer, Margaret spoke in coarse, guttural language of Boswell's life and work from 1775 until his death by lightning in 1831 at the Horncastle, Lincolnshire, fair. When the tape was played back at the end of the session, Margaret, thirty-six, "was totally unaware of anything she had said, and was astonished to hear that she had changed sex," said hypnotherapist Maurice Blake of Norwich, England. Margaret's next move was a pilgrimage to the neighboring county of Lincolnshire to see whether there was any truth to her ramblings. It wasn't long before she had the eerie sensation of standing next to the grave of Tyzo Boswell in the graveyard of St. Mary's Church at Tetford. The tombstone confirms that Boswell was "slain by lightening" [*sic*] on August 5, 1831, and the burial of his remains, two days later, is duly recorded in the parish register. Once on Boswell's home territory, Margaret felt great familiarity with her surroundings. "I'd never been to the area before," she said, "but I knew exactly where the grave was." Neither Margaret nor Maurice Blake had had the slightest contact with gypsy life and yet Margaret's regression was replete with Romany words, for example, "motto" meaning drunk, "mello" for dead and "chopping greis," meaning selling horses, all of which were later verified.

"The Reincarnation Experiments," a stunning television documentary in which four housewives from Sydney, Australia, gave details of past lives under hypnosis and then verified the evidence—in front of TV cameras and independent witnesses—by traveling thousands of miles to the scenes of these bygone lives, was screened before the Australian public in March, 1983. Even atheistic reviewers were compelled to admit that reincarnation appeared to be the only logical explanation for these remarkable journeys through time which followed hypnotic regression conducted by hypnotherapist Peter Ramster.

Cynthia Henderson, for example, who had voiced her past-life memories in colloquial French, led a film crew to a bomb-ravaged, 300-year-old chateau near the village of Fleur in Normandy—her home as French aristocrat Amélie de Cheville. The experience was so powerful that she burst into tears. Helen Pickering, another member of the experimental quartet, journeyed to Aberdeen where she had lived as James Archibald Burns, who had been born in 1807 in Dunbar, Scotland. While still in Sydney, Helen had drawn a detailed sketch of Aberdeen's Marshall College of Medicine that was verified by the only man alive who knows precisely how the building used to be, local historian David Gordon, collector of every plan and drawing from the college's beginnings. That a woman who had no access to his work and didn't even know the plans existed could possess such historical knowledge was "inexplicable," said Gordon. Inexplicable, that is, unless Helen Pickering walked the college's forgotten corridors and staircases as the medical student James Burns a century and a half ago. Aside from these structural revelations, Helen's recall of Burns' life was authenticated by records in the county library at Blairgowrie, the town where Burns had set up a successful medical practice.

Verification isn't always accomplished so easily. Most regression material doesn't contain the specifics sorely needed by researchers if only because the dates and the names of towns and streets usually lack the emotional charge that inspires recall. Also, most past lives, having been lived long before the establishment of Marshall McLuhan's global village, were so removed from the mainstream of history that even such basics as time period and country of origin would have been of little account to the ordinary person. Preoccupation with time is a modern development. Moreover, many nation-states have experienced frequent boundary changes. These difficulties are compounded by the fact that names and dates are stored in the speech centres of the brain, usually the left hemisphere in the temporal lobe, whereas sensory memory recall seems to be a function of the right hemisphere.

Reassuringly, there are ways to establish whether subjects are reporting from genuine altered states of consciousness and not merely spouting the wildest imaginings that enter their conscious minds. EEG (electroencephalograph) studies show that past lives are being tapped when brain levels measure 8.3 cycles per second. Flickering eyelids or REM (rapid eye movement) accompany this state. Some regressionists enlist the aid of a galvanic skin response device which records pore activity when wired to two of the subject's fingers. Once subconscious memory is reached, the device's needle moves away from the horizontal position. "It's like a very unsophisticated lie detector," said hypnotist John Hainlen, who finds his biosonometer has increased productivity at his Sacramento clinic. "If the conscious mind starts to interfere, we know at once."

As the journeying into past lives goes on, the search intensifies for more and better evidence to provide an unshakeable interpretation of the phenomena. Be that as it may, many of the researchers in the field have already convinced themselves that reincarnation underlies and makes possible the reams of testimony from other existences. Dr. Helen Wambach, who in 1975 resolved to determine whether past-life recall is fantasy or reality, says after regressing thousands of volunteers to past lives: "I don't believe in reincarnation—I know it." Ask her why and she'll reply: "If you are sitting in a tent on the side of the road and 1,000 people walk past telling you they have crossed a bridge in Pennsylvania, you are convinced of the existence of that bridge in

Pennsylvania." On the other hand, Joe Keeton, who has conducted more than 17,000 regressions and claims to have removed several cancerous conditions by hypnotic suggestion, can make no sense of the phenomena. "I'm just as puzzled now as when I started," he said. "I'll keep on prospecting till I die but I doubt whether I shall find the answer." Then he added: "Apples were falling off trees for millions of years before Isaac Newton came along and asked the right question. What we need are questions, not answers."

Not recommended for the faint-hearted, past-life excursions may help to ease discomfort, alleviate anxiety and enlarge understanding. And while some would say that to be a tourist of far memory is just another way of describing the self-examination of the psyche, what *is* the psyche but the sum total of an individual's experience in action? As Hazel Denning, president of the Association for Past Life Research and Therapy, points out: "You are everything you have ever been—right now."

6

So Long Ago:
The Roots of Belief

Rebirth is an affirmation that must be counted among the primordial affirmations of mankind.

CARL JUNG

The origin of the philosophy of reincarnation is prehistoric. It antedates the remotest antiquity all over the world.

E. D. WALKER

There was a time when all human beings, being clairvoyant, perceived the process of rebirth as clearly as they understood physical reality. Having a direct line to the supersensible worlds, people were fully aware of the cosmic circumstances, including the necessity of repeated earth lives. But somewhere in the lost reaches of prehistoric antiquity, having arrived at the crossroads of choice, humans elected to tread the path of spiritual degeneration—fossilized in legend as the Fall of Man—and gradually surrendered this preternatural power of clairvoyance. From then on, knowledge of reincarnation gave way to faith and to belief. This believing, a direct consequence of the fallen state, came to be known as religion, a yearning and striving for the sublimity that had been left behind.

Ancient myth and fable, tribal memory, lingering belief among adherents of the great religions and some grotesque archaeological discoveries all testify to ages long forgotten when reincarnation, much more than the intriguing conjecture it is today, was a commonly accepted law of life. Buried remains of Neanderthal society dating from roughly between 200,000 B.C. and 75,000 B.C., indicate the earliest known belief in rebirth. Skeletons have been found pressed into a flexed fetal position, as if in expectation of the next incarnation, with evidence showing that the deceased had been interred with supplies and sacrifices of animals such as bison and wild goats. Corpses were placed in line with the sun's east-west axis, hinting at recognition that the sun itself rises daily from the womb of Earth.

Shamanic belief, which reaches back into the Upper Paleolithic period between 15,000 and 25,000 years ago, held that the essential life force animating humans and animals resides in the skeletal form: it was from their very bones that creatures were reborn. An Aztec myth tells of a new human race being fashioned from the ground-up bones of the dead impregnated with blood drawn from the penis of the god Quetzalcoatl. And, as recently as this century, German ethnologist Leonhard Schultze-Jena when studying the Quiché Maya of Guatemala between the world wars, was told that the bones contain the vital essence of human life. Flesh, it was explained, is like the flesh of fruit that soon withers and decays, whereas the skeleton resembles the seed from whose tough shell life is born anew.

Across the world, legends of godlike men who managed to rise, in a state of perfection, to other realms of existence hark back to an era before human beings had cast away from the divine source. W. Y. Evans-Wentz, writing in *The Fairy Faith in Celtic Countries*, maintains it is logical to assume that there have been other human races in past aeons of time who have evolved completely out of the physical world into the divine plane of existence. "Hence the gods are beings which once were men, and the actual race of men will in time become gods," he declares. "Man now stands related to the divine and invisible world in precisely the same manner that the brute stands related to the human race."

A strikingly similar pattern of myth and legend, in which great kings and heroes were considered to be reincarnations of gods or divine beings from other worlds, is to be found in the records of ancient civilizations as diverse as Egypt, Britain, India, Greece and Latin America. To the Gaels and Brythons King Arthur was a reincarnated sun-god who had returned to educate and inspire the human race. In Egypt, the Pharaohs were thought to be divine appointments of Osiris, ruler of the underworld and judge of the dead. Among the Aztecs and Incas in the New World, the belief persisted that their great heroes had moved on to celestial lodgings in the sun which they would occasionally forsake to reclaim a body and renew the instruction of their people. In ancient Greece, Zeus, the mythological ruler of gods and people, was said to be reborn in the great national heroes that succeeded from age to age, Alexander the Great being one of them. The noblest inspiration in the venerable literature of India is attributed to such figures as Rama and Krishna who are both gods and men. "I produce myself among creatures," Krishna, masterful teacher of the Hindus, says in the Bhagavad-Gita, "whenever there is a decline of virtue and an insurrection of vice and injustice in the world; and thus I incarnate from age to age, for the preservation of the just, the destruction of the wicked, and the establishment of righteousness."

Countless echoes from the great tradition of reincarnational belief merge to form a global chorus of yearning for what has been and for what could be again. The richest voices in this wistful choir are those of the great initiates of India who, still in possession of the fading clairvoyance, poured their revelations into scripture. Although Hinduism, the oldest religion in the world, dates back to the fourth millenium B.C., reincarnation was not clearly enunciated in its teachings until the sixth century B.C. No one can vouch for the source of the doctrine, but it was supposedly handed down, not by the Brahmins, but by an older, red race who were kin to the ancient inhabitants of Egypt and Chaldea. The suggestion is made that their teachers were a race of demigods, or divine beings in human form, who might well have had their origins in Atlantis where reincarnation, it is said, was known rather than believed in.

The Wheel of Life

The pervasive Hindu belief in reincarnation holds that all human beings, animals, plants and minerals are strapped to the wheel of life which repeatedly turns its charges through revolution upon revolution of birth and death. The destiny of human beings, who are thoroughly responsible for their own rise and fall in this voyage of rotation, is dictated by their karma. This means that it is human actions that influence, for good or ill, not only personal fate but also the equilibrium of the universe. Karma has produced the present from the deeds of past lives, and prepares for eternity through the actions of today. The hope of Hindu believers lies in working through their karma so that they may attain eventual deliverance or *moksha* from the dread bondage of the wheel. However, the chances of such release are slim indeed, liberation being won only through immense difficulty. Again and again, desire for the sensuous pleasures of terrestrial life pulls the soul back to successive lives on earth. And being sinful, human beings cannot even be reassured that they will reincarnate next time in human form: severe transgressions can lead to rebirth as an animal just as an animal can succeed in winning a future life as a human. The rough road of consequences is sharply delineated in the *Svetasvatara Upanishad*, 5.11:

> As the body is augmented by food and water, so the individual self, augmented by its aspirations, sense contact, visual impressions and delusion, assumes successive forms in accordance with its actions.

The Lord of Death in the *Katha Upanishad* metes out a sardonic word of warning to those who hoodwink themselves with their own selfishness and seem to think they can avoid the repercussions that must follow:

> Ignorant ones, due to their deep attachment toward wealth and enjoyment, get deluded and blinded to

think that this planet alone exists and that there are no other *lokas* [dimensions]; that one need not think about any good actions or preparations for life after death for this Earth alone is everything and there is no other universe. Such foolish ones come under My rod again and again by revolving in the birth-death cycle.

So deep-seated is belief in rebirth among the hundreds of millions of Hindu worshippers today that, according to Nancy Ross in *Three Ways of Asian Wisdom,* "the idea of a succession of lives for each human creature would be no more debatable to the average Hindu than a Westerner's fixed belief that continuity from childhood to adulthood exists in a single life, even though the past may be largely forgotten." Such conviction is shared, moreover, by those who have chosen, or have been chosen by, the other great religion of the East, Buddhism.

The profound Buddhist teachings of reincarnation and karma followed the wisdom of the Upanishads within a century. To Gautama Buddha, who is believed to have lived from 563 to 483 B.C., reincarnation and karma explained the seeming meaninglessness of life and pierced the absurdity of all the apparent inequality in the world. Buddhism differed from Hinduism, however, in denying that there is a soul that persists from one incarnation to the next. The newly born human is the result of the preceding entity only so far as merging waves or candle flames bear relation to one another. For this reason, Buddhists prefer to term "rebirth" to "reincarnation," the Pali word for rebirth being *punabbhava*, which literally means "an existence again." Buddhists do maintain, nevertheless, that an individual's fundamental thought at death becomes the very thought that imbues the nucleus of the new existence.

Doctrinal idiosyncracies aside, the Hindus and Buddhists have similar conceptions of the painfully slow journey of purification from body to body. Craving and ignorance are the great obstacles to enlightenment and human beings, loath to change their ways, revolve incessantly on the wheel of rebirth, bound fast by the chains of karma. In the words of a Buddhist text:

> To be born here and to die here
> to die here and to be born elsewhere,
> to be born there and to die there
> to die there and to be born elsewhere—
> that is the round of existence.
>
> (Milinda's Questions, 77)

Gautama Buddha, who is said to have lived 550 previous lives over more than 25,000 years, stressed that attachment to earthly existence confined human beings to the treadmill of rebirth. Teaching that to give up clinging desire is to surrender the need to return, he told his disciples:

> For that which clingeth to another thing there is a fall; but unto that which clingeth not no fall can come. Where no fall cometh, there is rest, and where rest is, there is no keen desire. Where keen desire is not, naught cometh or goeth; and where naught cometh or goeth there is no death, no birth. Where there is neither death nor birth, there neither is this world nor that, nor in between—it is the ending of sorrow.

Long before the birth of Buddha, and even antedating its adoption by the Hindus, reincarnation was a central theme of the Eleusinian Mysteries which, named after the small town of Eleusis lying fourteen miles west of Athens, are traditionally thought to have originated as long ago as the fifteenth century B.C., before the Greeks had settled their native land. The mystery rites were strictly secret, but it is thought that by participating in a rebirth ritual, which sounds like an artificially induced precursor of today's much reported out-of-body experiences, neophytes were given glimpses of life after death and the onward momentum of the soul. At her loom, the goddess Persephone was said to weave new bodies for old souls. And, on Earth, some corpses were interred with special instructions reminding the souls they carried to ask for the water of remembrance that flowed from a spring in Hades. This would enable them to recall, in their next reincarnation, details of the life they had left behind.

Reincarnation, known by the Greeks as metempsychosis,

crops up again in the Orphic Mysteries of the seventh century B.C., with an Orphic text referring, in classical Indian fashion, to "the sorrowful weary wheel." The doctrine was antiquated indeed by the time of Pythagoras and Plato, though its age was anybody's guess. The Greek historian Herodotus, who lived in the fifth century B.C., pointed to the Egyptians as the first reincarnationists, while the Egyptians themselves acknowledged that the teaching had come out of the East in the unfathomable long ago. Their writings tell how the god Osiris, who personified esoteric knowledge, was driven to Egypt from India in the form of a spotted bull.

Whether the doctrine was likewise driven into Western Europe where the Druids, Celts and Gauls wove colorful rebirth tales into their fabric of mythology is beyond documentation. Suffice to say that there's a strong affinity between the Eastern round of existence and the circles of becoming described in the *Barddas* of the Welsh Druids. According to the *Barddas*, there are three life circles of which the intermediate, *Cylch Abred*, is the circle of rebirth. The soul dwells successively in each one, materializing in all possible forms of matter and spirit before entering a state of perfection and bliss comparable to the Indian *nirvana* which awaits those who finally manage to wrest themselves from the wheel of life. The ancient Europeans, it is said, were so confident of rebirth that they wept in commiseration at the birth of a child and greeted death with rejoicing. The Druids, in an even stronger statement of conviction, accepted that if borrowed money could not be repaid in this life, the debt could be made good in the next incarnation!

Orthodox Islamic, Jewish and Christian belief all deny reincarnation, yet each of these great schools of religious thought have accommodated streams of reincarnational teaching. Transmigration or *tanasukh* is viewed as inconsistent with the teachings of the prophet Mohammed, but the Koran says, quite explicitly:

> And Allah hath caused you to spring forth
> from the earth like a plant;
> Hereafter will He turn you back into it
> again, and will bring you forth anew—
> (Sura 71:17–18)

The wellspring of Judaism's esoteric mysticism is the Kabala and that is where reincarnation or *gilgul*, the Hebrew for "circuit" or "rotation," is to be found. Everything follows from the creation of a limited number of souls which gradually achieve purification and reunion with other purified souls. *The Zohar*, a Kabalistic classic believed to date back to the first century A.D., states:

> The souls must re-enter the absolute whence they have emerged. But to accomplish this end they must develop all the perfections, the germ of which is planted in them; and if they have not fulfilled this condition during one life, they must commence another, a third, and so forth, until they have acquired the condition which fits them for reunion with God.

Reincarnational teaching in the Bible is largely "taken for granted, cropping out here and there as a fundamental rock," to quote from E. D. Walker's classic nineteenth-century work *Reincarnation*. Several Biblical passages only make sense if they are interpreted in the context of repeated Earth lives. The following New Testament extract is one of several allusions to the same kind of hard-fought struggle for the godhead as that envisaged by the Hindus and Buddhists:

> Him that overcometh will I make a pillar in the temple of my God, and he shall go no more out.
>
> (Revelation 3:12)

Yet reincarnation spelled nothing but strife for the early church. Factions sprang up siding for or aginst the doctrine and, tragically, Christianity was turned into the battleground of a vicious, protracted dispute. The next chapter will examine the circumstances surrounding the withdrawal of Christian belief in reincarnation, a belief held strenuously by several early church fathers as well as the Gnostics (from the Greek *gnose*, meaning "knowledge") who prided themselves on seeking the inner, mystical meaning of the Christian message.

Tribal Memory

As religious belief in reincarnation was passed down from generation to generation in the old civilized world, tribal obsession with the very same idea, in differing forms, was rife across vast tracts of the inhabited territory that remained. Virtually all the tribal groups in North and South America, Indonesia, Australia, Asia and Africa lived with the conviction of immortality which, to most of them, implied reincarnation. "However it has been arrived at," wrote Sir James George Frazer in *The Belief in Immortality* (1913), "this doctrine of the transmigration or reincarnation of the soul is found among many tribes of savages; and from what we know on the subject we seem to be justified in conjecturing that at certain stages of mental and social evolution the belief in metempsychosis has been far commoner and has exercised a far deeper influence on the life and institutions of primitive man than the actual evidence before us at present allows us positively to affirm." Over the past century, tribal customs and traditions have been flouted as a result of the incursions of modern materialism, and often all that remain are stories and superstitions—the fading residue of a devout and binding creed.

One of the most commonly shared beliefs was that ancestors return to their families in succeeding incarnations. Among the Yoruba tribe of West Africa, a child born shortly after the death of a grandparent is still likely to be called *Babatunde*, meaning "Father has returned," or *Yetunde*, "Mother has returned." The Llo tribe of southeast Africa aim to find out exactly who is being reincarnated by repeating names of ancestors as soon as a new born baby is held to its mother's breast. The name being uttered at the instant the baby begins to suck is considered to be the relative who has returned. In a variation on this theme, bones held by members of the Yukagir of Siberia would suddenly decrease in weight when the correct ancestral name was mentioned, although today the deciding factor is the baby's first smile.

A custom widespread among North American tribes was to give a pregnant woman charms made of the hair of the dead relative whose rebirth was hoped for. In the Marquesas, a South Pacific archipelago where a grandfather's soul was thought to be transmitted into the body of his grandchildren, a wife who was having difficulty conceiving reinforced her chances of becoming a mother by placing herself under her grandfather's corpse. Among the Tlingit of Alaska there was even further communion with the dead. At the burial of a loved one, a pregnant woman of the tribe would hold one of the corpse's hands against her breast while wishing with all her might that her unborn child would inherit its spirit. After circling the grave eight times, she scraped a line leading about seven feet from the graveside. She then squatted to urinate at the end of this line and beseeched the spirit to be reborn through her.

Sometimes, the living made careful preparations for their own rebirth. It was customary for an elderly Inuit (Eskimo), sensing the beginning of the end, to approach a young couple in the neighborhood and request that he be reborn into their family. If he was a likable, respectable old gentleman, the husband and wife would probably tell him they would be delighted to have him for their first child. The elder, his destiny assured, would then await his death with patience and contentment.

In Northern and Central Australia the souls of the dead who were waiting to be reborn were said to haunt certain natural features of the parched landscape—a lone withered tree, say, or a pool of water at the foot of a ravine. The Aborigines, believing that every person is reincarnated, felt that these spirits were just waiting for a woman to pass by so that they could enter her womb. Knowing the spirits' preference for nubile maidens, young women who had no choice but to pass these landmarks but didn't want to become pregnant would make themselves look like old hags and hobble past, whining in a thin, cracked monotone: "Don't come to me. I am an old woman."

The mythical Rainbow Serpent is the Aborigines' link with the sky-world and symbolic maker of the road along which pre-existent spirits pass to the wombs of the mothers who will bring them back into the world. Often, the Serpent's huge body is pictured as a great conveyor of souls bound for rebirth. Some native Australians pin their hopes on reincarnating in the privileged white race. A black convict, about to be executed in Melbourne in the second half of the last century, went to his death full of such anticipation. "Very good!" he exclaimed. "Me jump up Whitefellow!"

Before immigration made white men a common sight in Australia, the Aborigines were convinced that pale-skinned visitors were reincarnations of their people. Not having any idea of leaving their own lands, they couldn't imagine others doing so and consequently believed that whites, in choosing particular locations, must have formed an attachment for these sites as dark-skinned tribesmen in a former existence. The explorer Sir George Grey told in his *Journals of Two Expeditions of Discovery in North-West and Western Australia* (1841) how he was "wholly unprepared" for the scene that followed the approach of an aboriginal procession led by two women whose cheeks streamed with tears:

> The eldest of these came up to me, and looking for a moment at me, said: *"Gwa, gwa, bundo bal"*—"Yes, yes, in truth it is him"; and then throwing her arms around me, cried bitterly, her head resting on my breast; and although I was totally ignorant of what their meaning was, from mere motives of compassion, I offered no resistance to her caresses, however disagreeable they might be, for she was old, ugly, and filthily dirty; the other younger one knelt at my feet, also crying. At last the old lady, emboldened by my submission, deliberately kissed me on each cheek, just in the manner a Frenchwoman would have done; she then cried a little more, and at length relieving me, assured me that I was the ghost of her son, who had some time before been killed by a spear-wound in his breast. The younger female was my sister; but she, whether from motives of delicacy, or from any imagined backwardness on my part, did not think proper to kiss me. My new mother expressed almost as much delight at my return to my family as my real mother would have done, had I been unexpectedly restored to her.

Scalping and cannibalism, two of the most brutal expres-

sions of tribal life, may well have been attempts to prevent
the reincarnation of the enemy. Hair had great significance to
North American Indians and a dead man without his hair
would be at a considerable disadvantage in the spirit world.
The primal idea behind cannibalism could have been the
absorption of the victim's soul matter, the aggressor taking on
the new strength of another soul even as he blocks his adver-
sary's chances of rebirth. The reasons why Peking man of half
a million years ago broke open the bases of skulls, presumably to eat the brains, are still being debated. Since the
discoveries were made at Choukoutien, a cave site in the
suburbs of Peking, archaeologists haven't been able to agree
on the nature of this custom. Were these early people trying
to assimilate the souls of their ancestors? Or were they performing some benevolent rite aimed at preventing rebirth?

The death of small children—common enough in the
Third World—was usually fraught with meaning. Stillborn
babies, for example, were thought by the African Ibo tribe to
be the outcome of one who decides, on entering a new life,
not to resume the struggle on the same old unhappy plane.
In many a primitive society, particularly in Northern India and
Central Africa, parents would bury a dead child under the
threshold of the family home in the hope that its returning
soul would be reborn to them. For the same reason, the Hopi
of Arizona made a road from the grave of the child to its old
home and the Canadian Huron Indians buried their babies
alongside a thoroughfare so that they would be reincarnated
in women who passed by.

But there were deeper, darker interpretations applied to
infant mortality—especially if a family was afflicted by the
death of one child after another. Either to induce the soul to
remain longer at its next incarnation or to discourage it from
making another attempt at rebirth, the bodies of children
who died young were subject to mutilation in parts of Africa,
America and India. Toes, legs and fingers were broken; faces,
noses and ears cut; and ears and fingers amputated. Sometimes, the mother would swallow a piece of lopped-off ear in
the hope of drawing the baby's spirit back to her body. And
in the dissimilar nations of Estonia and Nigeria, families
suffering a string of stillbirths shared the custom of burying

the most recent body face downwards in the hope that the errant soul would not see the way to be born again.

The Reverend John Martin, a Wesleyan missionary in West Africa from 1843 to 1848, witnessed a rowdy crowd carrying a very dirty-looking child about the streets of Accra in a basket. He wrote in his diary some time in 1845:

> On enquiry I learned that the mother had lost two or three children previously, who had died when about the age of this. When such is the case they believe that the same soul which was in the first child returns, and enters the next, and that the child, of its own will through mere spite, dies. Hence these steps are taken. The child while alive is besmutted with charcoal, put into a basket, and carried round the town, when the people take care to abuse it for its wickedness, and to threaten it, should it die. Every ill-usage that can be offered, short of murder, is shown it. Should it afterwards die, its head is sometimes crushed with stones and the body, refused a burial, is thrown either into the sea, or in the bush. These things are done to prevent its coming again in another child.

Death and rebirth pervade the ancient rites of initiation that reach back through the centuries in many parts of the world. Initiatory death was an indispensable preliminary to the awakening of spiritual life. In jungle and forest, initiatory cabins were built to signify personal and cosmological rebirth, the cabin representing "the maw of the devouring monster in which the neophyte is eaten and digested . . . [and] also a nourishing womb, in which he is engendered anew," writes Mircea Eliade in *Rites and Symbols of Initiation*. The initiatory hut, preserved in popular tales from Europe to New Guinea where a huge raffia dummy of a monster's belly called *Kaiemunu* is still constructed, reveals a periodic, primitive need to unify, if only briefly, human experience with cosmic grandeur.

But just how primitive is primitive? Perhaps the time-twisted legacy of tribal memory bears in its rites and rituals the seed of higher knowledge once known and now forgotten.

And perhaps we human beings, bound to the pendulum of evolution as surely as we are to the wheel of life, are even now on our way back to the garden. Whether or not we get there is up to us, as Pico della Mirandola observed at the close of the fifteenth century in his *Oration on the Dignity of Man*. He put these words into the mouth of the Creator:

> . . . We have made you a creature neither of heaven nor of earth, neither mortal nor immortal, in order that you may, as the free and proud shaper of your own being, fashion yourself in the form you may prefer. It will be in your power to descend to the lower, brutish forms of life; you will be able, through your own decision, to rise again to the superior orders whose life is divine.

7

The Lost Chord of Christianity

Reincarnation is assumed in the Bible teaching . . .
DICTIONARY OF ALL SCRIPTURES AND MYTHS

Put not off from day to day and from cycle to cycle, in the belief that ye will succeed in obtaining the mysteries when ye return to the world in another cycle.

JESUS CHRIST
(FROM THE GNOSTIC SCRIPTURE,
PISTIS SOPHIA)

Everyone knows the annals of religious history are stained with blood and corruption. Few appreciate, however, that the ruthless expulsion of reincarnation from Christian thought and theology has left some of the deepest and most shameful stains of all. Time has since worked its healing of forgetfulness and today most Christians are unaware that reincarnation was ever considered seriously by the church. But the fact remains that before Christianity became a vehicle for the imperial ambitions of Roman emperors, rebirth was widely accepted among the persecuted faithful.

Taught by a number of early church fathers and treasured by the Christian Gnostics, a movement in the apostolic tradition dedicated to preserving and promulgating the esoteric teachings of Jesus Christ, reincarnation was seen to be consistent with Old and New Testament scripture and complementary to the idea of personal salvation through Jesus Christ. From the earliest days of primitive Christianity, repeated earthly existences were a fact of life to many supplicants so long as they soldiered on in the quest for enlightenment. Yet they also believed that the monotonous cycle of birth and death could be transcended through the inspiration of Jesus Christ whose promptings towards spiritual perfection were able to exalt the individual to reconciliation with God and relief from the burden of the body.

The principal architect of this theological edifice was Origen, called "the prince of Christian learning in the third century" by St. Gregory of Nyssa, and hailed by the *Encyclopaedia Britannica* as "the most prominent of the church fathers with the possible exception of Augustine." While devoted to scriptural authority, Origen was also very much inclined towards the Platonic philosophy that had prevailed in Alexandria, the city of his birth, for more than four hundred years. He emphatically agreed with Plato that the divine eternal soul is cast into the corruptible body in order to prove itself superior to the inclinations of the flesh. Thus he wrote in a letter published in *A Select Library of the Nicene and Post-Nicene Fathers of the Christian Church:*

> If it can be shown that an incorporeal and reasonable being has life in itself independently of the body and that it is worse off in the body than out of it; then beyond a doubt bodies are only of secondary importance and arise from time to time to meet the varying conditions of reasonable creatures. Those who require bodies are clothed with them, and contrariwise, when fallen souls have lifted themselves up to better things their bodies are once more annihilated. They are thus ever vanishing and ever reappearing.

In *De Principiis*, his major work and the first systematic theology of Christianity, Origen declared:

> Every soul . . . comes into this world strengthened by the victories or weakened by the defeats of its previous life. Its place in this world as a vessel appointed to honor or dishonor, is determined by its previous merits or demerits. Its work in this world determines its place in the world which is to follow this.

For Origen, whose faith brought him torture and imprisonment at the hands of the Romans in the last years of his life, and for other church fathers such as Justin Martyr, founder of the first Christian school in Rome, the scriptures were to be interpreted in the most expansive, allegorical way. The visionary breadth of Origen's cosmic theology was not always appreciated by fundamentalists who cherished a narrow, literal reading of the scriptures. But the most telling opposition to the doctrine of reincarnation in Christian theology only developed once the church had evolved, in the fourth century, from harried bands of secret worshippers to an institution that could be exploited for political advancement and control.

The Abuse of Christianity

The seeds of reincarnation's banishment were sown when Constantine the Great, the first Roman emperor to become a Christian, perceived his faith as the reason for his military supremacy. Before triumphing over the mightier forces of Maxentius at the Battle of Milvian Bridge in 312, he saw a cross of light superimposed on the sun, a vision that led him to believe he was Christianity's chosen defender. As an expression of gratitude for this success, religious freedom was granted to all for the first time. And just as bemused Christians were beginning to accept that they were at last being tolerated by the authorities, Christianity was established as the state religion! Within twenty years, Christianity had progressed from an illegal cult, whose members were hounded, abused and exterminated, to the official religion of the empire. Yet there was a high price to be paid for the gifts and favors Constantine lavished on the church: the ecclesiastical rock was to be sculpted strictly according to the emperor's political designs. Ethics, faith and devotion became subordinate to the allure of personal interest and political power. Bishops were appointed not for their spiritual leadership but for what they could do to further Constantine's aim of unifying the empire. For the first time in history, the church began to attract nominal Christians, those who attended for social, economic or political reasons rather than for the pursuit of righteousness.

Eager to safeguard what he understood to be the authentic Christian message, Constantine kept up the political pressure by calling the Council of Nicea in 325 to determine and define Christian orthodoxy. From then on, the powerful union of church and state—always dominated by the emperor's wishes—decreed what was acceptable and what was heretical. Two lives were all that orthodoxy allowed—one life in the natural body and one hereafter in the form of resurrection. Bishops who disagreed with the council's findings, and there were some notable renegades, were quickly deposed. Meanwhile, those devout Christians who were disenchanted with the secularization of the church initiated their own monastic movement. Tending to settle in the deserts not so much to get away from the world as to escape the worldly church, they set themselves the task of trying to preserve the Christian prototype, a religion as pure and simple as the Savior's life.

This cleaving of the early church was accentuated in 380 when the establishment acted to outlaw and chastise free-thinking Christians. The Edict of Thessalonica, decreed by Emperor Theodosius without consultation with the ecclesiastical authorities, vowed that "all peoples who fall beneath the sway of our imperial clemency should profess the faith which we believe to have been communicated by the Apostle Peter to the Romans and maintained in its traditional form to the present day." The edict went further still . . .

> And we require that those who follow this rule of
> faith should embrace the name of Catholic Christian

adjudging all others madmen and ordering them to be designated as heretics, condemned as such in the first instance to suffer divine punishment and therewith the vengeance of that power which we, by celestial authority, have assumed.

In other words, heresy was no longer merely sinful; it was a crime, punishable by death. (Ironically, the word "heretic" means, at root, nothing more pernicious than one who is "able to choose.") In 385, the first of a long line of reincarnationist martyrs fell to the barbarism of the church-state alliance when seven Spanish adherents of the Priscillian sect were found guilty by a Christian magistrate of erroneous belief. Yet for another one hundred and fifty years or more, there was no official edict condemning the doctrine of reincarnation across the empire. These desert Christians, many of them Gnostics or, at least, subscribers to Origen's interpretation of the scriptures, led their lives with little interference from the prime movers of church policy. In the sixth century, however, increasing hostility towards Origen's teaching culminated in the Emperor Justinian being asked to adjudicate in a dispute between Origenist and anti-Origenist factions in Palestine. Justinian gave his answer by convening a synod at Constantinople in 543 which condemned the teachings of Origen. (There must have been little doubt as to the outcome because Justinian had, in 529, closed the University of Athens, the last stronghold of Neoplatonism and, as such, a centre of reincarnational study.) The emperor later issued fifteen "anathemas"—formal ecclesiastical curses involving excommunication—against Origen, four of which were aimed directly at pre-existence and, by implication, reincarnation. The first read:

> If anyone assert the fabulous pre-existence of souls, and shall assert the monstrous restoration which follows from it: let him be anathema.

It is thought that Justinian submitted these official curses to a preliminary session of the unconstitutional Second Council of Constantinople in 553. Pope Vigilius, who had been Justinian's prisoner for eight years, refused to participate in the deliberations and it was left to the attending bishops (representing, overwhelmingly, the Eastern church) to sanction the autocratic emperor's wishes. Although there is no evidence that the curses against reincarnation were even discussed at the full ecumenical gathering, historians have for centuries mistakenly assumed that the Second Council proceeded to adopt them. In a sense, however, the question of official ratification is irrelevant. What matters is that ever since the ecumenical council of 553, the church has shunned the doctrine of rebirth.

Just why belief in reincarnation incurred the wrath of institutional authority is open to interpretation. But it seems likely that reincarnationists caused greatest offence by their self-reliance, which had the effect of minimizing the sway of their totalitarian masters. Believers in reincarnation were neither to be induced by promises of heavenly bliss nor intimidated by threats of hellfire; they didn't need priests and ritual devices such as the confessional to guide them along the straight and narrow path to God. In toiling for their own salvation, they looked upon the church's cultivated dependence of the masses as unnecessary. And this left the church fiercely intolerant of professing Christians whose subservience could not be guaranteed. Writes Hans Holzer in *Patterns of Destiny:* "The church needed the whip of Judgment Day to keep the faithful in line. It was therefore a matter of survival for the church not to allow belief in reincarnation to take hold among her followers."

So it was that any departure from the official line was brutally punished by the guardians of orthodoxy. And yet, despite the menace of the most severe reprisals, including mass torture and execution, Christian sects clinging to their "heretical" beliefs proved themselves irrepressible. These sects were grouped together under the umbrella of Catharism (the religion of catharsis or purification), a term originally applied by St. Augustine to the reincarnationist Manicheans of Mesopotamia. The Cathars, who always believed themselves to be the true Christians, included the Paulicians of Thrace, the Bogomils of Bulgaria, the Patarenes of the Balkans and the Albigensians of southern France, while other groups flourished in northern Italy and Germany. Despite the fearsome vengeance of the Inquisition, which spared no effort to root out the rebels, Catharism "spread so rapidly and resisted so stubbornly the sternest efforts of suppression that at one time it may be fairly said to have threatened the permanent existence of Christianity itself," comments Henry Lea in his *History of the Inquisition of the Middle Ages*. Linked with the Cathars were the Knights Templars, a Christian military order founded to protect pilgrims visiting the Holy Land, and the troubadours, traveling minstrels who wandered around Europe between the eleventh and thirteenth centuries popularizing the doctrine of reincarnation in their ballads. Simple love songs acted as lyrical disguises for tales of how well-spent lives were rewarded by rebirth in bodies suitable for further spiritual development.

As the church's crusade of terror and slaughter was pursued to its bloody finale, the next life was increasingly all that was left to sing about. In 1244, the Albigensians were massacred to the last man, woman and child at their fortress of Montségur in the Pyrenees. The church councils of Lyons in 1274 and Florence in 1439 drove home Justinian's anathemas by affirming that souls go immediately to heaven, purgatory or hell. So thorough was the destruction of heretical works that most of what remains of Origen's disputed discourses is only available because it was quoted in the arguments of his opponents! And much of that was first "smoothed" by his Latin translator, Rufinus, who admitted that he didn't want to offend the church authorities. By the sixteenth century, reincarnational thinking had been routed from the public consciousness and the responsibility for smuggling the belief forward to the modern age was left to mystical groups such as the Alchemists and the Rosicrucians.

Biblical Testimony

Confirmation that reincarnation is indeed "the lost chord of Christianity" (a phrase attributed to William Q. Judge, a founder of the Theosophical Movement which has roots in Gnostic philosophy) can be found in the pages of the Bible. While the Old and New Testaments hardly trumpet the belief from the rooftops, there are numerous references to rebirth in both books. James M. Pryse asserts in *Reincarna-*

tion in the New Testament (1900) that to dispute that the doctrine is distinctly taught in the New Testament "is to deny that the authors of that collection of writings meant what they said in unmistakable language."

Several of the most explicit statements are made by Jesus Christ who affirmed his own pre-existence with the words "Before Abraham was, I am." (John 8:58) In the presence of a man who was born blind, Jesus was asked by his disciples: "Master, who did sin, this man or his parents, that he was born blind?" Jesus answered: "Neither hath this man sinned nor his parents: but that the works of God should be made manifest in him." (John 9:1–3) Although the disciples were clearly attributing prenatal existence to the blind man, Christ does nothing to correct or dispel this presupposition as he goes on to prepare a salve that restores the man's sight. By refusing to challenge the disciples' thinking, Jesus acknowledges the fact of pre-existence with its undeniable implication of reincarnation.

In the Gospel according to Matthew, chapter eleven, Jesus identifies John the Baptist as being Elijah reborn. Referring to the Old Testament prophecy that Elijah would appear before the coming of the Messiah, Jesus said: "This is he of whom it is written. . . . For all the prophets and the law prophesied until John. And if ye will receive it, this is Elias, which was for to come. He that hath ears let him hear." Further on in the gospel account, Jesus underlines this assertion by declaring that "Elias has come already." The disciples, Matthew points out, "understood that he had spoken of John the Baptist." Both men, being big, boisterous and frenetically inspired, not only looked and dressed alike but also possessed the same character traits. Certainly, anything less than the absolute fusing of Elijah's identity with John the Baptist undermines Christ's claims to be the Messiah. The poet Robert Graves commented in a *Playboy* article in December, 1967: "No honest theologian can therefore deny that his acceptance of Jesus as Christ logically binds every Christian to a belief in reincarnation—in Elijah's case, at least."

St. Paul's statement in his Epistle to the Galatians, ". . . whatsoever a man soweth, that shall he also reap" (Galatians 6:7) hints strongly at rebirth because one life is plainly insufficient for a perfect balancing of accounts. Likewise, verse ten in chapter thirteen of Revelation indicates karmic reprisal with all the portentousness of Hindu and Buddhist scripture: "He that leadeth into captivity shall go into captivity: he that killeth with the sword must be killed with the sword." Given that many soldiers die quietly in their beds, these words suggest that retribution must be experienced in a future life.

The rebirth of Jacob and Esau is mentioned several times in both the Old and New Testaments. Before the children were born, "neither having done any good or evil," God declares in Romans 9:13: "As it is written, Jacob have I loved but Esau have I hated."

To complete this Biblical selection is a prayer of Moses, evocative of cosmic timelessness as well as the recurring cycles of human beings and nature:

> Thou turnest man to destruction; and sayest, Return, ye children of men. For a thousand years in thy sight are but as yesterday when it is past, and as a watch in the night. Thou carriest them away as with a flood; they are as a sleep: in the morning they are like grass which groweth up.
>
> (Psalm 90:3–5)

If the Bible does little more than assume reincarnation this is because its contributors "might just as well give information regarding the digestive process, sleep or any other natural vital function," according to G. A. Gaskell's *Dictionary of All Scriptures and Myths*. More straightforward in its approach is the Gnostic gospel *Pistis Sophia* (meaning "knowledge-wisdom" and claiming to be the secret teachings of Jesus to Mary Magdalene) which quotes Jesus as saying that "souls are poured from one into another of different kinds of bodies of the world."

The Aquarian Gospel of Jesus The Christ, having been transcribed from the Akashic Records during the last century by Levi, a pastor and medical doctor of Belleville, Ohio, cannot be classed as having the same scriptural authority as gospels with historical pedigrees. Nevertheless, the authenticity conveyed by the pages of this psychically transmitted work extends to a reincarnational passage in which Jesus, after listening to a group of youthful singers and musicians in Lahore, makes the following comment:

> These people are not young. A thousand years would not suffice to give them such divine expressiveness, and such purity of voice and touch.
> Ten thousand years ago these people mastered harmony. In days of old they trod the busy thoroughfares of life, and caught the melody of birds, and played on harps of perfect form. And they have come again to learn still other lessons. . . .
>
> (Chapter 37:13–15)

Today's leadership of the Protestant and Roman Catholic churches, although by no means eager to consider reincarnational belief for Christian adoption, must be well aware of the growing empathy it generates in ecclesiastical circles. Perhaps this warming trend harks back to the conversion of the Reverend William Alger in the second half of the last century. An energetic Unitarian minister who devoted half his lifetime to a work on immortality called *A Critical History of the Doctrine of a Future Life,* Alger dismissed reincarnation as a plausible delusion in the book's first edition, published in 1860. But after further concentrated study he was so overpowered by the "peerless sublimity" of the doctrine that he gave rebirth his heartiest endorsement in the final edition, published in 1878. More recently, a number of leading clerics have spoken out in favor of reincarnation. In a 1957 lecture titled *The Case For Reincarnation,* Dr. Leslie Weatherhead, a former president of the Methodist Conference of Great Britain, declared:

> The intelligent Christian asks not only that life should be just, but that it shall make sense. Does the idea of reincarnation help here? . . . If I fail to pass those examinations in life which can only be taken while I dwell in a physical body, shall I not have to come back and take them again?

A 1979 survey by the University of Surrey sociology

department on attitudes among Britain's Roman Catholics reported that an astonishing twenty-seven per cent of Catholics believe in rebirth. An indication of the seriousness with which the establishment viewed this resurgence of the old heresy was the subsequent publication by the London-based Catholic Truth Society of a pamphlet titled simply *Reincarnation* by Father Joseph Crehan. Crehan states tersely: ". . . Our faith has no room for theories of reincarnation." Nor, it must be said, has the faith of fundamentalist Christians who, according to a September, 1982, editorial in the American magazine *Reincarnation Report*, are "using the same age-old manipulative fear-guilt-superstition formula to control the masses and perpetuate their own power."

The battlements of the old guard will always be vigorously defended. But there's no denying the undercurrent of partiality for reincarnation that could, unless confronted sympathetically, create quite a disruption in the halls of conformity. California theology professor Dr. Pascal Kaplan—who in 1972 was refused permission to write his Harvard doctoral dissertation on rebirth because, in the words of his rejector, "no-one connected with theology in the West since the third century has taken reincarnation seriously"—is fascinated by the recent surge of reincarnational interest. He points out that there's a growing network of priests, nuns and ministers who, in accepting reincarnation, believe that an understanding of rebirth "provides a framework for a deeper, truer understanding of their religion and of the essence of Christian spirituality." According to Kaplan, many advocates play "very significant" roles within the church hierarchy.

It may be just a matter of time before one of these individuals argues his or her position too loudly to be ignored by the establishment church, thus precipitating the public airing this bottled-up issue has long demanded. Meanwhile, the lost chord awaits its rehabilitation in the symphony of the ages.

8

The Bardo State: from Grave to Cradle

> *The past situation has just occurred and the future situation has not yet manifested itself so there is a gap between the two. This is basically the bardo experience.*
>
> CHOGYAM TRUNGPA, *RINPOCHE*

> *The Soul-Ego takes its flight into Dreamland.*
>
> MADAME H. P. BLAVATSKY

Across the threshold of death lies a realm beyond our conscious understanding, a fourth-dimensional commonwealth of spirit in which the human entity, released from bodily constraints, is steeped in the quintessence of being. Ancient Tibetans referred to this profoundly mysterious condition as the *bardo*, the plane of consciousness between lives. In the eighth century, Tibetan scribes compiled and condensed the out-of-body journeyings of generations into a guidebook mapping out the psychic territory to be negotiated once the body has perished. For centuries, the *Bardo Thödol*, better known to Westerners as *The Tibetan Book of the Dead*, has been recited into the ears of the dying and the deceased in hope of steering the liberated soul across the "dangerous ambush" of the *bardo* (literally, *bar*, "in between"; *do*, "island") and away from the necessity of rebirth.

According to *The Tibetan Book of the Dead*, the experience that lies in wait at death ranges over a symbolic forty-nine days, from blissful envelopment in "Clear Light" to the most terrifying, gory hallucinations. If the *bardo* traveller can only accept the absolute beauty and truth of the Clear Light or, failing this, if he or she refuses to be intimidated by the evil visions which, after all, are only born of personal *karmic* thought forms, then it is possible to merge with the Godhead and escape "the muddy swamp of *samsara*." Most human souls, however, are unequal to this task and gradually descend from the gloriously intense brightness that greets them at death to confrontation with their personal devils and, eventually, yet another earthly body. The three *bardo* stages in which self meets self in ever-degenerating encounters are. . . .

Chikhai Bardo: The supreme serenity of the between-life state is reached right at the beginning. Death yields to the Clear Light which is simply, if overwhelmingly, "the radiance of thine own true nature." The book describes the Light as being "like a mirage moving across a landscape in springtime in one continuous stream of vibrations." Everything, it seems, is bright, blissful and boundless. To quote the book once more, "all things are like the void and cloudless sky, and the naked, spotless intellect is like unto a transparent vacuum without circumference or centre." As welcome as this transcendent state must be, the Light usually overpowers the doubting, guilt-ridden human ego. And the consciousness principle falls away to the. . . .

Chönyid Bardo: Here, the living consciousness of the dead person views its abandoned body and, on hearing the mourning of friends and relatives, tries in vain to contact them. The discarnate entity experiences sounds, lights and rays which awe, frighten and fatigue the flagging soul surprised by its bodily transformation. Next come visitations from peaceful and wrathful deities—post-mortem dreams brought on by the karmic reflexes of actions committed in the physical world. In a sense, nothing has changed. The book intones: "As men think, so are they, both here and hereafter, thoughts being things, the parents of all actions, good and bad alike; and, as the sowing has been, so will the harvest be." Which is to say that if the previous life has been loving and honest, the hallucinations will be correspondingly heavenly; if nasty and deceitful, horrifying visions will rear up to match. Most people's lives will have been an amalgam of good and ill—hence the book's description of two kinds of projection. The wrathful deities are vile indeed; they advance tearing heads from corpses, drinking blood, and threatening all manner of infliction. And so to the. . . .

Sidpa Bardo: Much to its surprise, the entity finds it can "instantaneously arrive in whatever place" by traveling through rock-masses, hills or houses. But the soul is cautioned neither to desire these "various powers of illusion" nor to grieve for the loss of the body which, in any event, becomes more and more dim as the last life is left behind and the next life is approached. Pursuit by sounds and hallucinations leads to a confrontation with the Lord of Death, yet another psychological projection, who consults his Mirror of Karma "wherein every good and evil act is vividly reflected." In more contemporary terminology, this is where the individual reviews and judges the thoughts and deeds of the past life. At last, as the time for rebirth draws near, visions are seen of a man and woman in sexual union—the entity's parents in the forthcoming life. If about to be born male, the soul feels intense jealousy towards the father and acute desire for the mother; the reverse being the case if the future gender is female. This, in turn, thrusts the entity into the path leading to the womb to experience "self-existing bliss in the midst of the meeting of the sperm and ovum." Consciousness is cloaked in forgetfulness as the embryo grows and grows to emerge from the womb as a reborn human.

Until ten years ago, *The Tibetan Book of the Dead* was regarded by many as an instructive yet essentially symbolic allegory, as quaint, moralistic and old world as a fairy tale by the Brothers Grimm. But a burst of medical research into near-death and out-of-body experiences has justified a more literal interpretation of much of the *Bardo Thödol*, mainly because the testimony of modern accident victims and hospital patients who have come back from the dead bears near-identical witness to certain stages of the venerable *bardo* state. Studies by Dr. Elisabeth Kübler-Ross, Dr. Raymond Moody, Dr. Kenneth Ring and others demonstrate that the after-death state is alive with commonly reported phenomena —a powerful, welcoming Light, a sense of peace and timelessness, freedom of movement and the ability to travel through objects, increased clarity of perception, surprise at being out-of-the-body coupled with the capacity to see and hear people nearby, strange sounds, the granting of a rapid review of the life that has gone before, a loss of the fear of death combined with a heightened sense of purpose and the inadequacy of words to describe the overall experience. How humbling it must be for medical scientists to accept that these dramatic findings had been set down on parchment in remote Tibet more than eleven centuries earlier.

Dr. Raymond Moody marveled in *Life After Life,* his best-selling account of near-death research, that the correspondence between the early stages of death related in *The Tibetan Book of the Dead* and the reports of his subjects "is nothing short of fantastic." The obvious conclusion to be drawn from this tallying of testimonies is that the survivors of out-of-body experiences have ventured part way into the between-life state, their reports reflecting the earliest, predominantly positive aspects of the *bardo.* "What may happen *after* the initial stages of death . . . remains an open question," comments Dr. Ring. Yet many of the witnesses seem to have traveled far enough to become aware of the process of reincarnation. One of Ring's subjects, a man who survived a serious car accident, said:

> . . . I got to see a movie of basically my life, of what
> *had* happened and what *was* happening. It was like,
> I have a *mission* here to do, let's say, and I had a
> choice of what basically I call going on with the
> physical body or starting over again with a new one.

The woman who, according to Ring's statistical measuring gauge, had the most profound near-death experience of all his subjects, reported:

I really believe that death is just part of a continuous cycle. . . . Not an end *at all*. . . . I know that whenever I have another grandchild, I look at him and think, "Could you be papa? Could you be mama? *Who* could you be?" And it's very exciting.

After a cardiac arrest left New York film maker Victor Solow clinically dead for twenty-three minutes, he was revived by a medical team's final desperate effort. Formerly skeptical of any life beyond the grave, Solow related his *bardo* adventure in the *Reader's Digest* (October, 1974):

> There was no time for fear, pain or thought . . . I was moving at high speed toward a net of great luminosity. . . . The instant I made contact with it, the vibrant luminosity increased to a blinding intensity which drained, absorbed and transformed me at the same time. There was no pain. The sensation was neither pleasant nor unpleasant but completely consuming. . . . The grid was like a transformer, an energy converter transporting me through form and into formlessness, beyond time and space. . . . This new "I" was not the I which I knew, but rather a distilled essence of it, yet something vaguely familiar, something I had always known buried under the superstructure of personal fears, hopes, wants and needs. This "I" had no connection to ego. It was final, unchangeable, indivisible, indestructible, pure spirit. While completely unique and individual as a fingerprint, "I" was, at the same time, part of some infinite, harmonious and ordered whole. *I had been there before* . . .

Documented evidence from medical after-care is not all that points to the verity of the *bardo* state. In a study of 127 cases of spontaneous past-life memory reported in the book *Lifetimes*, New York professor Frederic Lenz noted that the occasional between-life remembrances of his subjects not only contained common phenomena in exactly the same sequence but were also "strikingly similar" to the death and rebirth process portrayed by *The Tibetan Book of the Dead*. The LSD experiments of Dr. Stanislav Grof show that many of his subjects experience vivid and profound rebirth visions much like those described in the *Bardo Thödol*. "The human unconscious, activated chemically, actually tends to enact spontaneously a powerful confrontation with death that can result in transcendence," Grof has written. With a little help from lysergic acid diethylamide, volunteers have sat through the most shattering hallucinations, seeing themselves wallowing in excrement, drowning in cesspools, crawling in rotting offal or slurping blood. Visions of murders, torture, mutilations, sadomasochistic orgies and cruelty of all kinds are commonplace. But there are also psychedelic blasts of brilliant white or golden light during which the subjects feel absolutely purified as they glide in a timeless, indescribably beautiful universe.

Varieties of transpersonal experience, which Grof defines as an expansion or extension of consciousness beyond the usual ego boundaries and the limitations of time and space, are also brought on by the hallucinogenics mescalin (the active ingredient of the peyote cactus) and psilocybin, derived from a mushroom, sacred to Mexican Indians, called *teonanacatl* or "the flesh of God." The anaesthetic ketamine hydrochloride has the power to transport its users into a bright world totally dissociated from the body. "It's impossible to describe," said a medical doctor who has experimented with ketamine. "The 'you' that you know is not there. You forget your name and identity. There's only experience—and it can be terrifying if you're unprepared." According to anaesthetist Dr. Howard Alltounian, who conducted ketamine experiments with his late wife, Marcia Moore, the drug opens up the mind to the larger designs of the universe. "We see the reasons for which we came to birth, why we had to die, and why we decided to be born again—and we know these reasons to be good," he said.

Clinical work with schizophrenics has led psychiatrists to conclude that their patients' visions often represent, not denial of death or wishful fantasy, but unadorned experiential reality. The actions of Old Testament prophets and yogis of the East also testify to communion with this state of being. While Ezekiel sometimes remained in a trance for days, and Daniel spoke of his visions throwing him to the ground and making him physically sick, advanced yogis have demonstrated their ability to leave their bodies at will, to exist for weeks without food and even to merge with water and flame. Prisoners and monks confined to solitary cells, explorers subsisting in conditions of extreme isolation and sufferers of epilepsy, which the Greeks called "the sacred disease" for its capacity to inspire body-free timelessness, have all experienced comparative states of higher awareness. They're all dipping into various levels of the *bardo* to be rejuvenated by the knowledge that rebirth proceeds from the very jaws of annihilation.

Just as modern scientific findings can be referred back for comparison to *The Tibetan Book of the Dead*, so the *Bardo Thödol* echoes the earliest experiences of nonphysical awareness; experiences that gave human beings their primal notion of heaven and hell. Shamanism, a primitive religious practice of the Ural-Altaic peoples of northern Asia, has long incorporated a profound rite of annihilation and rebirth at the core of its initiation trials. Novice shamans, willing themselves into trance, lie alone and close to death for between three and seven days. In this state, they suffer the most hellish visions, including personal dismemberment and the scraping of flesh from their bones, before receiving new flesh and blood, spiritual enlightenment and rapturous transport to the heavenly realms. The shaman's vision, to quote from Joseph Campbell's *The Masks of God*, reveals "that sense of an immortal inhabitant within the individual which is announced in every mystical tradition." This obscure dweller-in-the-body "neither dies nor is born, but simply passes back and forth, as it were through a veil, appearing in bodies and departing." There's substantial evidence that hallucinatory drugs have been used for millenia to encourage the onset of shamanistic perception. The *Rig-Veda*, India's earliest religious document, glorifies a psychedelic mushroom called *soma* and, during excavations of a shaman's grave at the New Stone Age settlement of Catal Huyuk in Turkey, pollen analysis revealed that psychedelic plants had been placed beside the medicine man's corpse.

The ancient Mysteries of the old civilized world were rife with death and rebirth rituals, and myth and fable from around the globe is colored with tales of that free-floating state after death where the human spirit has yet to shed the thoughts and appetites of the Earth-world but must do without the satisfaction afforded by the physical body. In Scandinavian mythology, for example, the *Song of Olaf Ostesen* conjures up graphic images of disembodied discontent:

> In other worlds I lingered
> Through the length of many nights;
> And God alone can ever know
> How great the sorrow of soul I saw—
> In Brooksvalin, where souls
> Are subject to the cosmic judgement.

A number of renowned historical figures, Cicero and Virgil among them, have written glowingly of out-of-body experiences. Cicero, having rejoined his frame with renewed vigor, wrote: "We at last possess reasons why we should live; and we are not only eager to live, but we cherish a better hope in death." Plato, in the tenth book of the *Republic*, recounts the legend of Er who, twelve days after being killed in battle, returned to life as he lay on a funeral pyre to tell of his adventures in the other world. Er observed how, after undergoing judgement, each soul was granted the opportunity to choose the form of its next incarnation, a selection process determined by the individual's wisdom, or lack of it. Plato writes: "Most curious . . . was the spectacle—sad and laughable and strange; for the choice of the souls was in most cases based on their own experience of a previous life." The choice being made, the souls drank of the River Lethe (Greek for "forgetfulness") which erased all conscious memory in readiness for the next incarnation. Such enforced oblivion crops up again and again as a between-life theme.

Jesus Christ in the *Pistis Sophia* speaks of the soul drinking from a cup "filled with the water of forgetfulness" and, in Chinese Buddhism, Meng P'o, the presiding goddess of the underworld, ensures that souls quaff a bitter-sweet broth to drown all memory of their previous existence before returning to earth. "Body," wrote the Greek philosopher Plotinus, "is the true River of Lethe; for souls plunged into it forget all."

Modern medicine might have discovered an explanation

for this amnesia in a hormone called oxytocin, which controls the pregnant woman's rate of labor contractions. Research studies have established that large quantities of oxytocin produce loss of memory in laboratory animals and cause even well-trained animals to lose their ability to perform known tasks. Because a woman's oxytocin floods her child's system it is not unreasonable to suppose that this natural drug flushes away memories of former incarnations along with conscious remembrance of birth. Not that smearing of the slate of memory doesn't occur in life outside the womb. The inability of keen-minded adults to remember their earliest years and the frequent loss of recall among the elderly is, perhaps, nature's way of imparting the relative insignificance of conscious memory.

From *Amenthe* to *Gusho*

All sorts of names and conditions have been ascribed to the between-life state, the popular conception of which is largely decreed by culture and custom. The ancient Egyptians spoke of sensitive souls passing through the gate of the gods into the *amenthe* where they dwelt in continuous pleasure until descending once more to animate a new body. Similarly, the Hebrews of old envisaged a spell in *pardish* or paradise—the place where fruit ripens and is gathered or, esoterically, where the spirit matures from seed sown in earthly incarnations. Souls whose time in *pardish* has nearly expired are given instructions for the next life, explains the *Zohar*, before being sent out "sorrowing in exile; to a place where there is no true happiness because only in the presence of God can this state be attained." The Australian Aborigines of Queensland's Pennefather River believe that between incarnations the spirit resides in the haunts of Anjea, a mythical being who causes women to conceive by putting mud babies in their bodies. To the Okinawans of the South Pacific the interim kingdom is called *gusho* to be entered on the forty-ninth day after death by spirits who, though fleeing their dead bodies, remain in their homes until this time. There's an intriguing parallel here with the *bardo*'s forty-nine stations of planetary existence. Be that as it may, the

Okinawans believe that the entity returns to earth within seven generations in the form of an individual closely resembling the previous incarnation. Not mind but spirit reincarnates, the mind being inherited from ancestors. Some spirits, nevertheless, remain in *gusho* indefinitely to act as hosts and tour guides for new arrivals.

More than one hundred years ago the Russian noblewoman Madame Helena Petrovna Blavatsky and her Theosophical movement rifled Eastern mysticism for two terms to describe the afterdeath state: *kama loka*, meaning the "plane of desire," and *devachan*, a Tibetan word meaning "the blissful." According to Theosophy, *kama loka* is the astral region penetrating and surrounding the Earth where the soul is purged of its impurities before rising to the unalloyed spiritual joys of *devachan* where it rests—for up to fifteen centuries, according to Madame Blavatsky—until being drawn back to the chores of earthly existence demanded by the ceaseless, universal law of *karma*. The between-life process, argue the Theosophists, is remedial, restful and beneficial, as vital to the spirit as sleep is to mortals. Were the adoption of another body to follow immediately upon death, the soul, being thus deprived of the necessary opportunity for reflection and consequent development of its higher nature, would soon become utterly exhausted.

Rudolf Steiner, who headed the German section of the Theosophical Society before founding the Anthroposophical Society based on his own metaphysical researches, also spoke of *kamaloca* (his spelling) and *devachan* as both essential and complementary to physical existence. For evolution to proceed, the body must be repeatedly eliminated. In Steiner's words: "In order to sustain consciousness and to keep it active, we have been continually destroying our corporeal sheath." In *kamaloca* (recognizable, though most inaccurately presented, as the Roman Catholic purgatory, says Steiner) the soul weans itself of all desires, appetites and passions. Here, every past-life deed committed in relation to a fellow human being is re-experienced as if the acting individual were that other person. Simultaneously, the soul is drenched in the "spiritual rain" of the sympathies and antipathies of higher beings who pass judgement on these deeds. All the while, the entity is passing through the planetary spheres where a vision is presented of all its previous earthly incarnations spread out in a tableau. Work then begins on the creation of the next physical body in exact accordance with the experience, lessons and karmic propensities assimilated from the past life. "Nothing that you can ever do on earth," Steiner told an audience in November, 1922, "can be as great and manifold as what you have to do when from the starry worlds you build this temple of the gods, the human body." Before the spiritual seed of the physical body descends to the parents who have been chosen to receive it, the soul is granted a vision of the life to come. Sometimes, says Steiner, this preview is so shocking that the self draws back in horror. Should this happen, the soul might never truly incarnate in the body it prepares for itself, an eventuality which can lead either to so-called prenatal defects or to epilepsy, which reveals lack of full control over the organism.

The *Bardo's* Duration

The time spent between lives seems to be as variable as the length of the lives themselves. Reports range from whistle-stops of several hours to extended settlements of hundreds of years. Those who suffer violent or otherwise premature deaths appear to return faster than those who die of old age, personal choice being the overriding factor in establishing length of residence in the immaterial world. When Seth, the famous spirit guide who communicates through the mediumship of author Jane Roberts, was asked by a minister to reveal what determines the time between incarnations, he replied:

> You. If you are very tired, then you rest. If you are wise, you take time to digest your knowledge and plan your next life, even as a writer plans his next book. If you have too many ties with this reality or if you are too impatient, or if you have not learned sufficiently, then you may return too quickly. It is always up to the individual. There is no predestination. The answers are within yourself then, as the answers are within you now.

Despite its obvious capacity to terrify, the *bardo* state is a most seductive realm. Dr. Raymond Moody tells how many people, having drifted free of the body, resist the return to physical existence. It must be wrenching indeed to leave a state of relaxation described enthusiastically by a racing car driver as one thousand times greater than that induced by a sauna and massage! Virginia Tighe, as Bridey Murphy, told of basking in "just satisfaction" in "a place of waiting" between lives where all have knowledge of the future. Chicago-born past lives specialist Bryan Jameison reports that most people he regresses to the interim are lulled by a euphoric, floating sensation, a feeling of being surrounded by soft clouds. "Some people go over and find pure energy and light," commented hypnotherapist Dr. Edith Fiore. "And yet I have many who say they see beautiful lakes, beautiful scenes, gleaming cities. . . ." After such an abundance of sweetness and light, the sexual vortex that draws the soul back to the physical plane— described by a subject of German hypnotherapist Thorwald Dethlefsen as "the big vacuum cleaner"—comes as a jarring shock. Consequently, it's hardly surprising that Dr. Helen Wambach's research subjects, who report the average time spent in the *bardo* is fifty-two years, speak of birth being pervaded by an abiding sense of sadness and dislocation. As much as they would like to stay, the patients of Dr. Morris Netherton are rarely allowed to linger in the between-life state because, for all its mystery and promise of sudden revelation, he finds that nothing can be accomplished there to improve the present-life situation. In a pessimistic aside on the perversity of the species, Netherton writes:

> We are no different out of the body than in; unwilling to learn from our in-the-body experience, we repeat our patterns out of the body, until we can find a body to enter that will allow us to repeat in-the-body patterns all over again.

But if a person's mental traits and limitations are borne out of incarnation by the self, so the between-life state has continuing application to physical existence. It was always the intention of the Tibetan sages that the *Bardo Thödol* serve as much as counsel to the living as a guidebook for the dying.

Chogyam Trungpa in a modern commentary on *The Tibetan Book of the Dead* pursues this theme by remarking that the *bardo* experience is part of our basic psychological make-up. At every moment, birth and death are recurring. In fact, the *bardo* state could be said to be the experiences of paranoia and uncertainty in everyday life; feelings of not being sure of our ground, of neither knowing what we have asked for nor what we are getting into. More emphatically, states Trungpa, the *bardo* experiences can be seen "purely in terms of the living situation."

The unbodily rapture of the between-life state, it must be stressed, is simply the manifestation of a higher level of consciousness. William James, the American psychologist who used nitrous oxide and ether to "stimulate the mystical consciousness in an extraordinary degree," wrote that our normal waking consciousness "is but one special type of consciousness, whilst all about it, parted from it by the filmiest of screens, there lie potential forms of consciousness entirely different." Unfrequented, except in dreams, by the majority of the human race, these other realities are there *all the time* and can be experienced voluntarily by those rare beings who are spiritually self-realized. Some pay a visit with the help of drugs; others get there through hypnosis or by plumbing the deepest meditative states or, without wanting to, through schizophrenia or extremes of illness and isolation. And then there are those accident victims for whom traumatic flirtation with death leads inadvertently into the *bardo*. The rest of us, waiting patiently until our time expires, at least have something to look forward to—a sustained cosmic adventure that, in dissolving mortality's frustrating limitations, surveys the grandeur of innermost being.

9

The Ghost of
Future Past

*The Oversoul is before Time, and Time, Father of
all else, is one of His children.*

RALPH WALDO EMERSON

*. . . One level out, you see that who you are isn't
moving in time. Time is describing the incarnations,
the packaging changes.*

RAM DASS

Sometimes, thinking obstructs understanding: that's the
way it is with human conception of time. Thought, being
sequential by nature, presents the three-dimensional world
in terms of past, present and future—an interpretation that is
convenient, essential, even, for coping with the physical world.
But time, being a product of our mundane consciousness, is
no more than a convenient illusion. Visitors to the *bardo*
state, as we have seen, are well aware that time doesn't really
exist. Freed momentarily from the Earth-plane, they know
that everything is happening at once. As confusing as this
might sound to an aging individual watching the seconds tick

by on the clock surmounting a local historical monument, everything *is* taking place in the eternal *now*. Past lives, therefore, are transpiring simultaneously; only thought's way of viewing the world informs us otherwise.

Although wise men from Huang Po to St. Augustine have remarked on the unreality of time, reason has always balked at surrendering the linear view. Ken Wilber writes in *The Spectrum of Consciousness*:

> Thought is sequential, successive, one-dimensional, while the real world presents itself as a multi-dimensional, non-successive, simultaneous pattern of infinite richness and variety; and trying to make the one grasp the other is like trying to appreciate a beautiful landscape by looking through a narrow slit in a fence or trying to take in a Renoir painting by microscope alone.

Only when memory is no longer imagined to be real knowledge of the past but, instead, is understood to be current experience will the time illusion evaporate. Because the present moment contains all time, it is therefore timeless. And this timelessness is eternity. Of course, it is much less taxing to abide with past, present and future, but a more than superficial understanding of reincarnation insists upon broader horizons. As René Guénon declared: "He who cannot escape from the standpoint of temporal succession so as to see all things in their simultaneity is incapable of the least conception of the metaphysical order." Joan Grant, an Englishwoman whose far memory has recalled a long succession of past lives, does her best to make this idea of simultaneity easier to grasp by suggesting that time be seen as the centre of an orange, equidistant from its segments which are likened to the soul's various lives. Consequently, for Miss Grant, ". . . it is no more difficult to recall an episode which took place several millenia ago than to recall one from the current or the preceding century." Subjects regressed to former existences also find that recent lives are no more vivid or emotionally intense than those from the deep past. Seth, the spirit guide who appeared earlier in these pages, hammered home the eternal present's relevance to reincarnation in this communication:

Because you are obsessed with the idea of past, present and future, you are forced to think of reincarnations as strung out one before the other. Indeed we speak of past lives because you are used to the time sequence concept. . . . You have dominant egos, all a part of an inner identity, dominant in various existences. But the separate existences exist simultaneously. Only the egos involved make the time distinction. 145 B.C., A.D. 145, a thousand years in your past and a thousand years in your future—all exist now.

The illusory nature of time is perhaps best perceived by thinking of dreams which can telescope the experience of years into seconds. No time whatsoever passes for the dreamer. Nor, indeed, for one who is asleep or under hypnosis. Why? Because the inner self lives outside the temporal state. In the same way, a helicopter pilot lives outside the vehicle he is observing far below on a traffic-jammed highway. Suppose the pilot is the oversoul while the driver of each vehicle is a separate ego-soul experiencing a different life. The oversoul, being in the timeless state, can see all the various lives happening at once, but the separate souls, restricted in visibility and awareness, can see only their particular traffic problem.

The approaching years, with all their events, may be out of sight but only in the same way that higher vibrations of sight, sound, smell, taste and feeling are beyond the limitations of physical consciousness. The future is here and has always existed. That is why gifted clairvoyants can foretell what will come to pass; by psychically tuning in to a higher frequency they are able to perceive the everlasting present. Alan Vaughan, the editor of *Reincarnation Report*, argues in a February, 1983, article that the more we know about this "future," the better our chances of making the best choices in the present moment:

By learning more about our unconscious blueprint of life, we bring to the surface more of our reasons for choosing to be born. We can never, I suspect, know *all* of our blueprint, for that would remove our zest for life. In fact, the reason for the barrier between our unconscious and conscious minds may well be to prevent foreknowledge from completely robbing us of the thrill of our daily encounters.

Future Lives

Hypnosis, nevertheless, is able tp pierce the barrier cleaving the conscious from the unconscious. Theoretically, this means that, for a skilled hypnotist, future lives are no more inaccessible than past lives. Practically, however, progressions aren't conducted nearly so frequently as regressions. Future lives are impossible to document; information doesn't flow as readily and subjects, once adrift in the future, tend to switch spontaneously from one scene to another. Perhaps the mind, conditioned to see the future as forbidden territory, tries to block or jumble the store of images.

Dr. Helen Wambach recently undertook a pilot study called "Mass Dreams of the Future" in which hypnotized subjects were carried forward to the years 2100 and 2300 respectively. Eighty-nine out of 1,100 participants found themselves incarnate in one or both of the designated years and went on to describe "remarkably common" experiences. "Many more *wanted* to go into the future," said Dr. Wambach, "but they found they were not humanly alive in these time periods."

Perhaps they were not alive because of a dire shortage of bodies to accommodate them. The study pointed to a 95 per cent reduction in the earth's population by the year 2100 when subjects reported they were living in the aftermath of widespread destruction. The planet had been rendered barren and poisonous with roughly half of those alive in 2100 describing life in domed cities which they could leave only by donning a form of gas mask. One domed city was reported to be in Arizona; another in Tunisia. The other half of the population lived as space colonists eating mushy, artificial food with the aid of a strange utensil shaped like a fork and spoon combined. All vegetables had disappeared, but so had pain, violence and disease. By the year 2300, the subjects testified, vegetables had reappeared, people were living all over the solar universe and earth's population had doubled.

Progressions conducted by Dr. Bruce Goldberg, a Baltimore hypnotherapist, have encountered none of this apocalyptic material—at least, not until the twenty-fifth century when a major nuclear war apparently causes a "tremendous decrease" in the world's population. The "numerous consistent observations" reported by Goldberg in his book *Past Lives, Future Lives* range from major geographical changes during the next century to underwater cities and information pills in the twenty-sixth century. On February 2, 1981, Goldberg hypnotized Baltimore television newscaster Harry Martin and asked him to "read" the news one week hence. The WBAL newscast of February 9, 1981, showed that Martin had scored a number of minor successes, including a near-identical description of a road accident in the Baltimore area. Later, Harry Martin was moved forward to a life in the twenty-second century where he saw himself working as a scientist inside a solar-powered glass pyramid. Not a word is spoken among the three hundred people who live inside the pyramid; their appointed task is to explore thought transference. Progressed to the last day of this future life, Martin describes a high-tech version of euthanasia which he understands will lead to his rebirth:

GOLDBERG: Where are you?

MARTIN: I'm reporting to the termination room.

GOLDBERG: Are you still in the pyramid?

MARTIN: Yes.

GOLDBERG: Why are you in the termination room?

MARTIN: It's my turn to change units.

GOLDBERG: Can you describe this procedure?

MARTIN: I lie down on a table and they put something on my fingers and you just go to sleep.

GOLDBERG: What does this do to you?

MARTIN: It takes all of your energy out of you.

To dwell on the subject of progression is to addle the mind. Dick Sutphen, who has progressed subjects as far as the year 4000, once mused that, in different bodies disseminated across the future, people are probably interacting with many of the same souls they knew in past and present incarnations. And in 1976 he speculated: "Could it possibly be that, somewhere in time, my future self is being regressed to 1976 to find out about his spiritual roots? I wonder. . . ."

Time is freely given to all who accept the doctrine of reincarnation. And that's very attractive to people only too conscious of their limitations and shortcomings. For if perfection is beyond all reasonable expectation in this life then there's always the next existence, and the one after that. . . . With time and rebirth operating in tandem, there is no goal that cannot be reached; no virtue that can remain forever unattainable. An old Buddhist tale hints at the enormity of time required for expeditions of multitudinous incarnations. An image is presented of a granite mountain six miles high, six miles long and six miles wide. Every hundred years a bird with a silk scarf in its beak flies past this mountain, running the scarf over the rockface. The time it takes for the silk scarf to wear away the mountain is likened to the dimension of our being in round after round, in form after form, on plane after plane.

Yet if time doesn't exist, has anything really changed? Perception, that is all. Rational order falls away to the grandest vision imaginable. And the sands of timelessness are seen to be even more vast and imponderable than the sands of time.

10

Lesser Lives: Rebirth in the Lower Kingdoms

We can only get away from this necessity of an animal past by denying all soul to subhuman nature.

SRI AUROBINDO

A stone I died and rose again a plant,
A plant I died and rose an animal;
I died an animal and was born a man.
Why should I fear? When was I less by dying?

JALALU' L-DIN RUMI

Divine spirit, says the ancient wisdom of the East, permeates all matter. Manifesting as units of consciousness, this spiritual power embarks on an immense journey of progressive embodiment. Incarnation after incarnation as various minerals is followed by innumerable lives as plants followed by successive births and deaths as animals. When, at last, the human form is attained, the relentless cycle won't be stilled. Time rolls ever onward, fertilizing unto eternity the seeds of rebirth.

What Eastern sages had to say about the ascending consciousness of this Great Chain of Being was echoed by the *Barddas* of Celtic antiquity, a document which expounded a scheme of evolution in which the monad or soul passes through every phase of material embodiment before entering the human kingdom. The Rosicrucians, a mystical order of indeterminately ancient origin, have long held that every mineral contains an "eager fire" or "jewel of light"—the essence of evolutionary development. Furthermore, the findings of modern science support these claims that consciousness abides within all types of corporal envelopes. IBM scientist Marcel Vogel has shown through infrared photography that quartz crystals store and release energy, and he has also demonstrated that crystalline growth can be modified by human thought patterns. Various experiments have shown that plants are "living, breathing, communicating creatures endowed with the personality and attributes of soul," to quote from *The Secret Life of Plants* by Peter Tompkins and Christopher Bird. As for animals, their possession of mental and emotional faculties is self-evident; the nonphysical difference between the human and animal kingdoms being intellectual rather than spiritual.

At first glance, however, this progression of consciousness is hard to accept on sheer numerical grounds. The mind wrestles with an image of, say, trillions of sand-grain souls competing among themselves for the eventual tenancy of a lone human body. Yet the apparently prohibitive logistics of funneling the vast soul matter of minerals into plant existences and henceforth into the less plentiful bodies of animals and humans is explained by Manly P. Hall, president-founder of the Philosophical Research Society based in Los Angeles. He argues that only the physical aspects of minerals, plants and animals are individualized, their entity and mind being collective. Whereas humans must grow separately, the types and species that comprise the lesser kingdoms develop through the evolution of group consciousness.

Dorothy Maclean, whose psychic communication with plants was one of the major inspirations behind the spectacular Findhorn community in the north of Scotland where enormous flowers and vegetables flourished on land that had harbored only gorse bushes and spiky grass, has the same perception of the group soul concept. Writing of this woman's

emarkable ability to converse with plants for the betterment
f their welfare, Paul Hawken, in his book *The Magic of
Findhorn*, noted: "It became apparent that what was coming
through was not a spirit attached to one particular pea plant
r tomato bush but rather a spirit which was the plan, the
mold, and architect of all peas on the Earth."

The various natural kingdoms are linked by what Manly
Hall calls pronounced "transitorial forms." Between the mineral and the plant there are lichens and mosses; between the
plant and the animal there are certain carnivorous plants as
well as plants with elementary nervous systems. Between
animals and human beings lie the anthropoids and between
human beings and the next order stand the great initiates and
teachers—the demigods of classical antiquity.

Confirmation of our animal heritage can be found not
only in Charles Darwin's *Origin of Species* but also in the
case histories of past-life therapists, many of whom find that
patients, if carried back far enough in an altered state of
consciousness, will feel and see themselves in animal bodies.
Dr. Morris Netherton says that whenever he delves into the
earliest source of a patient's particular problem that patient
"almost always" describes an animal wound or death. Lying
on the couch in Netherton's office, people commonly regress
to lives as rodents, shrews, insects and, every so often, prehistoric creatures. Many of Joe Keeton's subjects do likewise.
Among the most convincing re-enactments he's observed have
been those of a woman who saw herself covered in reddish-
brown fur and lying under a boulder; another who envisaged
herself picking insects from a dead tree trunk; and a builder
who told of being close to the ground and covered in scales.
Although Dr. Helen Wambach hasn't tried to retrieve data
from animal lives, some of her subjects have found themselves on four legs whether they like it or not. "They look
down and see their little furry paws," she says.

Participants in Dr. Stanislav Grof's LSD experiments
have also reported identification with various animal ancestors. These feelings of identity usually apply to other mam-
mals, birds, reptiles, amphibians and various species of fish.
Grof says that his subjects can have "illuminating insight into
what it feels like when a snake is hungry, when a turtle is
sexually excited, or when a salmon breathes through its gills."

Less frequently, plant and mineral existences are related
Grof's subjects have experienced themselves as germinating
seed, as roots reaching out for nourishment and as the con
sciousness of such material as diamond, granite and gold
"Similar experiences," he writes, "can reach even the
microworld and depict the dynamic structure of the atoms. . . ."

The Laws of Manu

Once human, is it possible to be reborn into lesser lives?
The Hindus of antiquity believed that people lacking in vir
tue would surely be reincarnated as beasts and the dread
Laws of Manu spelled out precisely how this involution could
occur. Manu, a legendary legislator and saint who lived more
than two thousand years ago, decreed that each person's life
was influenced by one of three overriding qualities—goodness,
activity or darkness. Those endowed with darkness, which he
defined as the craving after sensual pleasure, were destined
to be reborn as some form of animal, insect or plant. "In
consequence of attachment to the senses, and in consequence
of the nonperformance of their duties, fools, the lowest of
men, reach the vilest of births," Manu declared. And he gave
pointed examples of the specific deeds that lead to particular
bodies of the lower kingdom: thieves of grain become rats,
thieves of honey, stinging insects; thieves of milk, crows,
thieves of meat, vultures. The "violator of a guru's bed"
enters a hundred times the forms of grasses, shrubs and
creepers. A woman who is "disloyal to her husband" is born
in the womb of a jackal—the list of crimes and punishment
goes on and on.

In the old days, Brahmin priests found the Laws a great
help in enforcing caste practices; there was nothing quite like
the threat of subhuman rebirth to encourage obedience. But
modern Hindus tend not to take the Laws of Manu quite so
literally, preferring to believe that base appetites and inclinations, rather than individual souls, are reincarnated in animal form. They argue that as neither plants nor animals are
capable of degenerating into lesser species, human beings,
though they might lapse into a savage state, must never be
less than human.

The ancient Hindus—who believed there were 8,400,000 different kinds of births culminating in the human race—were not alone in anticipating lower lives. The Buddhists held a popular doctrine of rebirth in subhuman realms which may well have led them to institute the first hospitals for the care of animals. Initiates and adepts of the faith, however, regard this teaching to be symbolic rather than literal, believing that karmic hardship can be experienced more profitably in renewed human form. They would rather not accept, at face value, the warning in *The Tibetan Book of the Dead* that when a bestial birth is imminent, the soul ". . . will see, as if through a mist, rock caves and holes in the ground and straw huts."

In ancient Egypt, magic spells from *The Egyptian Book of the Dead* were buried with the newly deceased so they would be empowered to change themselves into "whatever form they please." The Egyptians believed they must spend a cycle of 3,000 years migrating from species to species before they were finally able to be reborn as human beings. This idea resurfaces among the Inuit. Dr. Hartley B. Alexander in his *North American Mythology of Arctic Tribes* tells how souls may be reborn as both human and beast "and some have been known to run the whole gamut of the animal kingdom before returning to human shape."

The unenviable fate of King Nebuchadnezzar is central to the Jewish tradition of transmigration. The Book of Daniel (4:33) describes how the King "was driven from men, and did eat grass as oxen, and his body was wet with the dew of heaven, till his hairs were grown like eagles' feathers and his nails were like birds' claws." In the Kabala, the souls of the wicked were said to migrate into animal bodies—an adulterer, for example, was destined to pass into the body of a stork as it was believed that storks punish adultery with death. Moreover, the mixing of various seeds and the crossbreeding of animals was prohibited so as not to cause suffering to the souls they contained.

The Greek thinkers were similarly captivated by rebirth as an agent of human degeneration. While Plato explained the evolution of birds and animals by saying they arose from the deterioration of human souls, Pythagoras was said to have exclaimed on hearing the yelping of a beaten dog: "Beat him no more! His soul is my friend's as I recognized when I heard his voice." But it was Plotinus, the founder of Neoplatonism, who, like Manu, dared to be most explicit about the kinds of bestial bodies that would result from human actions and desires:

> Those who have sought only to gratify their lust and appetite pass into the bodies of lascivious and gluttonous animals. . . . Those who have degraded their senses by disuse are compelled to vegetate in the plants. Those who have loved music to excess and yet have lived pure lives, go into the bodies of melodious birds. Those who have ruled tyrannically become eagles. Those who have spoken lightly of heavenly things, keeping their eyes always turned toward heaven, are changed into birds which always fly toward the upper air. He who has acquired civic virtues becomes a man; if he has not these virtues he is transformed into a domestic animal, like the bee.

In the first century before Christ, the Roman poet Ovid put himself in the place of a victim of transmigration in penning his poem *Metamorphoses*:

> I am ashamed to tell you, but I will tell—
> I had bristles sprouting on me.
> I could not speak, but only grunting sounds
> Came out instead of words.
> I felt my mouth grow harder.
> I had a snout instead of a nose,
> And my face bent over to see the ground.
> My neck swelled up with great muscles,
> And the hand that lifted the cup to my lips
> Made footprints on the ground.

Early English and Scottish ballads rhapsodize about the souls of men and women migrating into various animals, birds or plants, and Breton folklore speaks of the spirits of fishermen and sailors materializing in the bodies of white seagulls. Seagulls themselves are remarkably eloquent on the subject of reincarnation as Richard Bach illustrates in his ever-popular novel *Jonathan Livingston Seagull*. Sullivan the gull is talking:

> Do you have any idea how many lives we must have gone through before we even got the first idea that there is more to life than eating, or fighting, or power in the Flock? A thousand lives, Jon, ten thousand! And then another hundred lives until we began to learn that there is such a thing as perfection, and another hundred again to get the idea that our purpose for living is to find that perfection and show it forth. The same rule holds for us now, of course; we choose our next world through what we learn in this one.

Understandably, the concept of human beings reappearing with cloven hooves, sharp beaks, shaggy thighs or any other animalistic appurtenance has always been a favorite butt of merriment, even among those sympathetic to the idea of reincarnation. William Shakespeare seized upon the theme in *Twelfth Night*, causing Malvolio to poke fun at the Pythagorean idea "that the soul of our grandam might haply inhabit a bird."

Scoffers come and go, yet the belief lingers on. Today there are millions of people from widely divergent cultures who remain convinced that humans can and do reincarnate as lesser beings. Residents of Japan far from the sprawling urban centres still hear in the plaintive singing of the pine insect the voice of the loved one who has been reborn among the bushes of the fields. On the Micronesian island of Yap, souls of the recent dead are said to come back as small, shining cockchafers. In March, 1975, villagers in central Sri Lanka refused to help the island's archaeological department drive away hornets that swarmed around an ancient rock fortress during excavations. Their reasoning was simple: they believed the creatures to be reincarnations of the soldiers of King Kassapa I who had guarded the fortress in the fifth century.

Five years earlier, in Glasgow, Scotland, Mrs. Josephine Ralston had watched a starling swoop down to attend her daughter's wedding service. Later, she declared: "I have never been more certain of anything in my life. That starling was my husband, George." According to Britain's *Weekend* magazine, George Ralston, who had died two years earlier, had often told his wife: "I believe in reincarnation. If I come back to Earth it will be as a bird." The starling not only perched beside Mrs. Ralston for most of the service but also fluttered to join the bride and groom at the altar and later followed the wedding party into the vestry for the signing of the register. As the congregation dispersed, the bird flew to a tree outside the church, chirped loudly, and flew away.

Thousands of miles away on the "Roof of the World," a fly falling into a cup of tea is seen as a catastrophe by Tibetans, according to Heinrich Harrer. The fly "must at all costs be saved from drowning," he writes in *Seven Years in Tibet,* "as it may be the reincarnation of one's dead grandmother. If at a picnic an ant crawls up one's clothes, it is gently picked up and set down." During Harrer's stay, a national decree was issued forbidding the general construction of buildings because worms and insects might easily be killed as work progressed!

Then there's the tragic story of fifteen-year-old Steven Shea who, in the spring of 1976, plunged fifty feet from a multi-storey car park in his home town of Letchworth, England. In his diary police found the clue to his bizarre death—a passage from Richard Adams' *Watership Down,* the best-selling novel about life in a rabbit warren, and a note which read: "I'm going to kill myself and become a rabbit." Yet Steven's obsession for transmigration into an animal body as splashed across British newspapers under the headline, "Tragedy Of The Rabbit Fantasy Boy" is not so extraordinary when placed in farthest historical perspective.

No Eastern religion developed a wider world view around the idea of reincarnation than that of the Jains of India who teach that everyone passes through literally millions of earth, water, plant, fire, wind, insect, animal and human incarnations. The water incarnations alone—each of which could last from less than 1 second to 7,000 years—range across seas, lakes, rivers, rains, dew, hoarfrost, snow, hail, ice, clouds and fog! Believing that every jot of matter accommodates living spirits trapped by their own misdirected will in the cruel round of rebirth, the Jains adopted the philosophy of *ahimsā*, or noninjury, towards all living things. Their exaggerated regard for life is maintained to this very day and devout Jains are expected to follow *ahimsā* to its minutest detail, with no concessions; for example, they may not kill any grubs found in vegetables.

Western tourists in India are puzzled by the tedious progress of white-garbed Jain monks who, wearing masks to prevent murderous inhalations, are careful to whisk away all possible insects from their path. The most pious Jains decline to travel by car because of the havoc wreaked on insect life and they arrange, when ascending mountains designated as shrines, to be carried aloft in sedan chairs by Hindu bearers whose regard for life doesn't extend to the meticulous preservation of the gnat, grub and beetle populations.

Vegetarianism rests on the principle that living creatures infused with divine spirit should not be consumed by human beings. Imagine, then, the plight of Burmese fishermen whose very livelihood runs contrary to their nation's religious tradition. In the social scale, only an undertaker has more difficulty in marrying off a daughter than a fisherman whose misdeeds are destined to bring him back to earth in one of the lower, probably aquatic, realms. Because necessity long ago demanded that they rationalize their lot, the fisherfolk, rather than killing fish and incurring punishment in the next life, merely place their catch on the riverbank to dry. Should the fish be unfortunate enough to expire during the course of this operation, so be it. The fishermen, at least, can't be blamed! Goverment officials ducked responsibility in the same way when Burma was under military rule in the late 1950s. When soldiers attempting to clear stray dogs from the capital city of Rangoon were ordered to place poisoned meat along the major streets by night, pure meat was prudently mixed with the tainted variety. In this way, the dogs were granted the opportunity to exercise free choice and their killers were acquitted of any violation of Buddhist law.

Shamans of the Cherokee Indians devised an equally ingenious way to pardon the tribe's hunters for killing animals for food. After assigning to every animal a definite lifeterm which could not be curtailed by violent means, the shamans ruled that, should any animal die prematurely, the death is only temporary. The body would be resurrected immediately from spilled blood drops to renew its existence until the close of the predestined period.

Tigerish Appetites Among the Tupinambi

Deep-rooted in the lore of African and South American tribes is the belief that one's enemies can reincarnate in the bodies of wild beasts. In Latin America, the most feared form adopted by reborn adversaries is the South American tiger or jaguar. Sixteenth-century Peruvian historian Garcilasso De La Vega wrote of jaguar-worshipping tribes whose members would offer themselves unresistingly on encountering the beast. Speaking as if they were these jaguars reborn, cannibals have been known to explain their fondness for human flesh in terms of tigerish appetites. Explorer Hans Staden, held as a slave among the Tupinambi of the Brazilian coast many years ago, described a grim visit to his Indian master:

> He had before him a great basket of human flesh, and was busy gnawing a bone. He put it to my mouth and asked if I did not wish to eat. I said to him: "There is hardly a wild animal that will eat its kind; how then shall I eat human flesh?" Then he, resuming his meal, said: "I am a tiger, and I find it good."

The Zulus accepted that their dead pass, according to rank, into various kinds of serpents and lizards. The Betsileo of Madagascar—who tied nobles' corpses to the central pillar of the family hut and allowed them to putrefy—believed that serpents called *fanany* were formed in a pot placed beneath the dead body. The soul-bearing infant *fanany* was carried to the tomb after the human remains had been buried and, several months later, a full-grown python emerged to be treated like royalty. The souls of ordinary members of the Betsileo was assumed to pass into crocodiles while any undesirables in the tribe languished as eels. A common practice among the Bagesu and Wanyamwesi tribes of East Africa was to throw out their dead to be devoured by hyenas. Consequently, the cry of a hyena in the evening was always fraught with meaning—it was the voice of the last person who had died in the neighborhood.

Native belief has not always required human souls to migrate into animal bodies. In many parts of the world, animals are thought to reincarnate as their own kind just as regularly. In fact, when food is at a premium, the pressure is on for human beings to do all they can to hasten this process. To this day, fish bones are thrust into the pole walls and palm-leaf thatch of homes belonging to members of the Warao tribe of Venezuela. This architectural contribution is made out of respect and anticipation, for it is believed that from the old bones new fish will be born. To ensure their salmon supplies remain plentiful, the Kwakiutl Indians of British Columbia take great care to throw the bones and offal of gutted fish back into the sea so that the reincarnating salmon soul is able to reanimate them. Setting fire to the bones, they strongly believe, would eliminate the possibility of rebirth. The Hurons and Ottawa Indians never burned their fish bones for the same reason, fearing they would antagonize the fish souls and drive away from their nets the embodied fish that remained.

The Eskimos of the Bering Strait, believing that seals, walrus and whales remain attached to their bladders after death, practised a ritual to speed up the rebirth of game so essential to their survival. Hunters carefully removed and preserved the bladders of all the sea beasts they killed, presenting them at a solemn annual festival. After being honored with dances and offerings of food, the bladders were taken outside and thrust through the ice into the frigid water. By returning the bladders to the sea, the tribesmen imagined that the souls of animals, flattered by such gracious treatment, would return willingly in new bodies for a fresh round of spearing and harpooning.

Haeckel's Law

Instincts of activity and migration point to animals, birds and fish repeating patterns learned over many lives. After four generations of being removed from nesting materials

African weaver birds, for example, are still capable of constructing nests that only their species can create. And freshwater eels, salmon and steelhead trout migrate to the identical rivers which served as home to their forebears, being drawn through rivers and oceans, one can suppose, by long-inculcated awareness of chemicals, temperature, velocity and direction. But it is Haeckel's Law that most implies reincarnation from the standpoint of biological science. Named after a German scientist of the past century, this law states: "In the ontogeny, the phylogeny is recapitulated." This is to say that during the earliest formative stage of any individual life there are a series of body changes which reflect the evolutionary history of the species. Each stage in the development of the human embryo is an awe-inspiring recapitulation of forms corresponding to unicellular protozoan life, jellyfish, worms, gill-bearing reptiles and apes! Most biologists attribute this progressive development to programming within the genetic material. But in so doing they deny the spiritual component which surely resides at the very heart of the chemical process.

It is said that the soul's experience in recent lives is reflected in human beings and beasts alike. Paying allegiance to this principle, Himalayan yogi Sri Swami Sivananda (1887–1963) has stated emphatically that pampered pets reveal themselves to be humans who have taken a tumble on the evolutionary staircase. He wrote:

> Some dogs get royal treatment in the palaces of kings and aristocratic people. They move in cars, eat good food and sleep on cushions. These are all degenerated human beings.

Swami Sivananda and those of similar persuasion are in the minority, however. Most professors of the soul hold that unremitting upward momentum is inherent to spiritual and physical evolution. This would indicate that animals endowed with special qualities of affection, loyalty and intelligence have almost attained the human level whereas people with brutish natures have joined the family of humans fresh from bestial existence. Sybil Leek, the British-born witch who died in Florida in 1982, had this to say about savages, criminals and loutish personalities in general:

. . . When we meet people who "behave like animals," we can perhaps understand them better if we view them as recently evolved egos who have just made it to the human kingdom. They are like children in a kindergarten who cannot be expected to understand, much less follow, all the rules that man in his evolution has learned.

Rebirth, as a means of dispelling ignorance and provoking understanding, is the key to the continuity of this learning. To be born once is to open one's books; to be born many times is to undertake a course of instruction. Only through repeated births can there be growth and consolidation, the fulfillment of promise, the granting of spiritual significance to otherwise meaningless innovation. The greater the number of incarnations, the better the individual's chances of understanding the plan behind the process. And as surely as birth follows death, human respect for life in all its forms advances with the developing awareness of our furthest beginnings.

The Climb to Superconsciousness

But where is all this evolution leading? From minerals to plants to animals to humans . . . to what? Just as a rock is brushed by swaying foliage yet cannot divine its sensibility, so we are blindly rubbing shoulders with our future. That future lies in the development of superconsciousness, a state beyond the pull of bodily reincarnation. It's conceivable that the denizens of this New Tomorrow of the mind will look upon humans in much the same way—though, one would hope, with greater compassion—that humans regard animals. Presumably, on some other plane of supersensible reality, Tomorrow is already here with the human race, even now, impaled like a butterfly specimen under its successor's gaze. That gaze would take in the interminable recurrence of the same old mistakes leading to the same old suffering. And yet, like the animal kingdom, the human race cannot be expected to evolve, of itself, into a state of perfection. Progressive stages of development satisfy that requirement. The human race can be compared to a class in school that will never improve in overall performance because those who learn their lessons move up to be replaced by others from a lower grade. The graduates, according to the discarnate Frederic Myers, a former Cambridge University classics professor who, after his death in 1901, communicated his experiences to mediums in different parts of the world, gradually evolve through the higher planes, passing beyond matter and form to dwell "not only outside of time but outside of the universe" and to become one with God.

As farfetched as such celestial peregrinations might appear, they are surely no more impossible than the human procession from the mineral kingdom. Evolution will not be constrained by our narrow-minded image of ourselves. Wrote Sri Aurobindo, India's late master yogi: "The soul is not bound by the formula of mental humanity; it did not begin with that and will not end with it; it had a prehuman past, it has a superhuman future."

11

Fearless Fighters and the Suicide Fallacy

He is not slain when the body is slain.

BHAGAVAD-GITA (2:20)

Suicide thwarts the plan of the entity which sends out the personality. . . . Fortunately the entity is far beyond the reach of man's destructive tendencies. . . .

MANLY P. HALL

Because he knows no fear, the warrior who believes in reincarnation is the most indomitable of fighting men. So visceral is his acceptance of rebirth that he can wade into the most frightful carnage confident of emerging spiritually unscathed. No matter how threatening or disadvantageous the battle situation, his inner composure will not falter. For the man who goes to war *knowing* he will return to earth is, in a sense, already dead inside. Resigned to the unthinkable, he has surpassed a purely intellectual understanding of reincarnation; he has plunged into the very process itself.

History teems with fearless fighters who have literally laughed at death. Buddhist tradition holds that reincarnation originally belonged to the warrior caste who guarded the doctrine from misappropriation by the masses. The Celts, the Druids, the Essenes, the ancient Germans and Scandinavians, many North American Indian tribes and, more recently, the Japanese in World War II, were all emboldened by the reincarnation connection. Each step towards death brought the next life a little closer, a life that could only be enriched by the valor, suffering and sacrifice of the present moment.

All who saw these campaigners in action and lived to tell the tale marvelled at their fortitude. Struggling against the Romans during the first century A.D., the Essenes, a monastic order living in Palestine, impressed the Jewish historian Flavius Josephus with their capacity to be "above pain, by the generosity of their mind." He wrote in *The History of the Jewish War*:

> They smiled in their very pains and laughed to scorn those who inflicted torments upon them, and resigned up their souls with great alacrity, as expecting to receive them again.

While others fight for life, warriors who embrace reincarnation fight for their lives. The twin exhorations of destiny and just cause override the karmic inadvisability of taking human life to inspire poised, purposeful fanaticism. It was this fanaticism that unnerved Roman legionnaires, in Britain under Suetonius Paulinus in A.D. 61, who were charted with subduing the rebellious Celts and Druids. Sounding as though he is relating nightmare images, the Roman historian Tacitus described the ghoulish reception that awaited the advancing Roman army on the sacred Isle of Mona, now called Anglesey:

> On the shore stood the opposing army with its dense array of armed warriors while between the ranks dashed women in black attire like the Furies, with hair disheveled waving brands. All round, the Druids lifting up their hands to heaven and pouring forth dreadful imprecations scared our soldiers by the unfamiliar sight . . .

In ancient Celtic mythology, the corpses of slain warriors were thrown into a cauldron of rebirth from which they arose refreshed and ready for renewed fighting. They were, however, unable to speak, which might well have been a symbolic way of communicating that the ordinary soldier, remembering nothing of his previous incarnation, was incapable of voicing his experiences. While Julius Caesar, the great Roman general and statesman, noted that the Celts were "in a great degree excited to valor" by the fearlessness that stems from belief in reincarnation, the Roman poet Lucan was clearly envious that the Druids were unmoved by the greatest human fear of all, the fear of death. "Hence their warrior's heart hurls them against the steel," he writes in the *Pharsalia*, "hence their ready welcome of death, and the thought that it were a coward's part to grudge a life sure of its return."

It's no accident that the dialogue of the Bhagavad-Gita, the great Hindu scripture suffused with rebirth teaching, is conducted on the battlefield. For the message of reincarnation is never more immediate or more pressing than when human life is at stake. As opposing armies mass on the field of Kuruksetra, Lord Krishna advises his friend and devotee, Arjuna, that there is no birth and death for the soul which "can never be cut into pieces by any weapon." Urging dauntlessness in the cause of religious principles, Krishna instructs his disciple:

> Only the material body of the indestructible, immeasurable and eternal living entity is subject to destruction; therefore, fight, O descendant of Bharata.
> (Bhagavad-Gita, 2:18)

Many North American Indian warriors were instilled with similar conviction of their perpetuity. To die honorably in combat was to ensure a happier rebirth, Indian lore being laden with accounts of slaughtered braves who have returned to life. In 1873 the French anthropologist Alphonse Pinart explained the "extraordinary fierceness" of the Tlingit Indians of British Columbia in recording that, rather than fearing death, they sought it out "fortified by the expectation of soon returning to this world and in a better position."

Hoaxed By Mythology

Ironically, the very creed which made the Indians so implacable in local battles sapped their resistance at the most critical junctures of history—when they were under attack, in various parts of the Americas, from European adventurers. Ancient legends prevalent the breadth of the continent had told for centuries of the return of the "dawn heroes" said to be of fair complexion, mighty in war and destined to recover their power, glory and lands of old. Initially, therefore, the pale-skinned invaders of the New World, instead of encountering unified opposition, were received with bemused wonderment which sometimes erupted spontaneously into joyous welcome. No wonder the Aztec and Incan empires toppled so precipitously to the imperialist ambitions of a few heavily armored Spanish ruffians! On the Eastern seaboard of the United States, the Maryland Indians fell victim to the same mythological hoax. They convinced themselves that the white men landing on their shores were the reborn representatives of a long-lost generation bent on reclaiming territory that once was theirs.

Reincarnation in the proud Japanese fighting tradition is a cry of defiance swelled by the most fervent longing to serve the fatherland forever. Rebirth to the warrior of Japan is *Shichishō Hokoku* or *Serve the Nation for Seven Lives*, a slogan which adorned the white headbands of *kamikaze* pilots in the final stage of the Second World War. This rallying shout of determination and derring-do—more an ardent desire for rebirth than a deep-seated conviction of its reality—dates back to the fourteenth century and the noble failure of the samurai Kusunoki Masashige, faithful servant of the Emperor Godaigo. Masashige had masterminded victory after victory against superior forces, culminating in the Battle of Minato River in 1336 when his troops were hopelessly outnumbered. Towards the end of the conflict, Masashige, bleeding from eleven wounds, limped from the battlefield with his younger brother, Masasue, to a nearby farmhouse to commit *hara-kiri* and thus avoid capture. As they were about to disembowel themselves, Masashige asked his brother what his last wish might be, to which Masasue replied: "I should like to be reborn seven times into this world of men so that I might destroy the enemies of the Court." Delighted by this answer, Masashige is said to have expressed the same wish before committing suicide.

So it was that the *kamikaze* pilots, faced with similar hopelessness in war, adopted identical yearnings in their suicidal missions against American warships in the Pacific. "You are already gods, without earthly desires . . . ," they were told by Vice-Admiral Takijiro Onishi, the man most responsible for initiating the suicide strategy. The pilots, most of whom were aged between twenty and twenty-five, volunteered readily for what was considered the privilege of *rippa na shi*, the "splendid death." Pleading to be dispatched into the skies and pouring out their thanks to senior officers when selected, they savored in advance the exquisite moment of self-immolation as plane and pilot, diving at 570 m.p.h., slammed into the steel-hulled target, furiously ablaze. That was the dream. In reality, however, the single-seater *kamikaze* planes, their noses packed with high explosives, often missed the aircraft carriers' afterdecks and were swallowed up in the ocean. Yet, for the pilots, effectiveness was always subordinate to honor. Before flying to his death on October 28, 1944, Matsuo Isao of the Heroes' Special Attack Unit wrote:

> I shall be the Emperor's shield and die cleanly with my squadron leader and other friends. I wish that I could be reborn seven times, each time to smite the enemy.

By the war's end, some 5,000 Japanese had died in various *kamikaze* craft—planes, launches and manned torpedoes. But they weren't the only fearless fighters from the Land of the Rising Sun clinging passionately to their ideals. In battle after battle in the Pacific War, Japanese soldiers avoided surrender by launching fierce, suicidal attacks. Perhaps the most fearsome scenes of all took place on the island of Saipan in July, 1944, when 3,000 Japanese, armed only with bayonets or sticks, charged into the concentrated machine-gun fire of the American marines. Wave after wave surged forward only to be mown down by the deadly hail of bullets.

At intervals, new machine-gun emplacements had to be found because Japanese corpses were piled so high they were blocking the lines of fire.

Notwithstanding the end of hostilities and the emergence of Japan as a powerful industrialized nation, the "seven lives" spirit, though fading, was not allowed to perish. Yukio Mishima made sure of that. The country's foremost novelist of the modern age, Mishima railed publicly against the erosion of patriotism in Japan, and wrote fiction which often had a reincarnational theme. In his last work, a series of four novels called *The Sea of Fertility*, the protagonist reappears in successive books as the reincarnation of the hero who has gone before, his identification being three moles on the side of the chest that endure from lifetime to lifetime. Even as this work was being written, Mishima organized his own private army called the *Tatenokai*, or Shield Society, with the aim of protecting the emperor from the threat of communism. On November 25, 1970, Mishima and four student members of the *Tatenokai* took an army general hostage at the military base at Ichigaya. There, wearing his *hachimaki* or headband emblazoned with the war cry *Serve the Nation for Seven Lives*, Mishima strode onto the balcony overlooking the parade ground to address a hastily convened gathering of soldiers on the subject of declining national values. Then he retired to commit *hara-kiri* before the captive general. Like Masashige and the suicide pilots who had preceded him, Mishima was in love with reincarnation, his will was strengthened by the idea, but it remained more of an impassioned hope than a belief. The last note this tragic Japanese hero left on his desk said it all: "Human life is limited, but I would like to live forever."

The Revolving Door

Torn between indigenous Shintoism's honorable death and the reincarnational pulse of imported Buddhism, Mishima would have refrained from taking his life had he truly believed in rebirth. For all the courage that *hara-kiri* demands, reincarnationists warn of the karmic repercussions that flow from self-destruction. In countries where the population at large believes in reincarnation, suicide, being regarded as a petty injunction against cosmic law, is rarely attempted. For it is felt that the problems that precipitate such an act of desperation cannot be avoided; they will only regroup to launch another, perhaps more serious, attack in another existence.

The great Russian writer Leo Tolstoy remarked in his diary:

> How interesting it would be to write the story of the experiences in this life of a man who killed himself in his previous life; how he now stumbles against the very demands which had offered themselves before, until he arrives at the realization that he must fulfill those demands.

Perhaps it is the return of these onerous pressures, made weightier still by the burden of self-murder, that creates the tendency for suicide in one life to be succeeded by suicide in the life that follows. Dr. Ian Stevenson reports the bizarre case of Brazilian Paulo Lorenz who claimed to be the reincarnation of his dead sister, Emilia. Emilia killed herself by taking cyanide on October 12, 1921—fourteen months before Paulo's birth. For the first four or five years of his life, Paulo wore girls' clothes, played with girls and with dolls and even shared his late sister's sewing skills. He also took on Emilia's self-destructive instincts. Paulo made several attempts to kill himself before committing suicide on September 5, 1966, by splashing inflammable liquid over his clothes and body and setting himself on fire. Stevenson noted in *Twenty Cases Suggestive of Reincarnation*: "In several other cases in which the related previous personality had committed suicide the subject has shown an inclination to contemplate and threaten suicide."

As much as the suicidal personality feels able to escape the world by getting rid of the body, reincarnation's revolving door ensures that all hope of dissolution is short-lived. Those who learn, under hypnosis, that they have killed themselves in past lives are quickly brought to the realization that suicide, far from being an answer to life's problems, is, at best, a stalling tactic born of ignorance. In *Reincarnation as a Phenomenon of Metamorphosis*, Guenther Wachsmuth describes the suicidal act as the violent breaking of the lifeline "on the basis of a knowledge of a fraction." And he adds that, if the perpetrator could only realize the resulting intensification of difficulty which must enter the life to come, such interference would never be countenanced. Yet there are those for whom belief in reincarnation actually *encourages* the act of suicide. Mental health expert Dr. J. William Worden, assistant professor of psychology at the Harvard Medical School, cites several cases in which individuals have decided to take their own lives believing that a better life awaits them next time around! While it seems highly unlikely that self-destruction should be rewarded with contentment, psychics and clairvoyants generally agree that death brings no reprieve from suffering, no matter how weary of life those who kill themselves might be. The between-life experience is thought to be characterized by a strong sense of physical deprivation because the suicide's spiritual and physical selves are not ripe for separation. Thus begins a fruitless search by the grieving entity for the body so suddenly withdrawn.

The unabating popularity of suicide (28,100 successful suicides and some 2,000,000 failed attempts in the United States in 1981) and the proliferation of suicide manuals in the Western world over the past few years, demonstrate that both mystical insight and scientific evidence into the postmortem state are being hugely disregarded as the act of suicide becomes more and more socially acceptable. The most blatant of the "how-to" guidebooks, a French publication titled *Suicide: Operating Instructions*, equates suicide with revolt against the established order—a more profound statement than the author intended—and even explains how to forge doctors' prescriptions for lethal drugs. An official of *Search*, a French suicide-rescue organization, condemned the manual with these words: "It's criminal. It goes against all our efforts. We're about rebirth. Their message is to flee from life."

How to stifle the self-destructive impulse? The only lasting antidote lies in the recognition that life, not oblivion, waits beyond the last heartbeat. As seductive as suicide might be to the deeply despairing, evolution will not be denied so presumptuously.

12

Pluto: Planet of Rebirth

Pluto kills or destroys but builds out of the elements of the destroyed—out of the old, something new . . .
FRITZ BRUNHÜBNER

Pluto can call for a drastic showdown.
ALEXANDER RUPERTI

Suspended in celestial deep freeze, the planet Pluto sweeps steadily across the outermost reaches of our solar system. Barely blessed with sunlight, this pale, mysterious orb is the most forbidding, most inaccessible planet known to humanity. Inhospitable is too kind an adjective for a world with little or no atmosphere, a craggy, cratered surface packed with ice and methane frost and an average temperature of minus 346° Fahrenheit. Remote is too gentle a delineation for this refrigerated oath of the Almighty banished to eternal rotation in deep space. Even when at its closest to the sun, Pluto is well over *two billion miles* distant, registering but a faint and yellowish stellar image through the lenses of the most powerful telescopes.

Pluto was discovered as recently as 1930, at the depth of the Great Depression. Since then, astronomers have tended to preoccupy themselves with the riddle of the planet's origins while astrologers have considered this invisible glimmer in the night sky from a completely different perspective. They dwell on its significance for the race. Pluto, they say, is the harbinger of death and rebirth; Pluto is coming into its own; Pluto is casting a lengthening shadow upon the affairs of human beings. As ruler of death and rebirth, Pluto is recognized to be a particularly potent force during those rare ages when the planet is at large in Scorpio, its own sign of the zodiac and the sign of sex and death. As this book goes to press the world is advancing to the brink of such an epoch. Pluto enters Scorpio on August 27, 1984, and there it will remain until November 10, 1995.

Profound global change—physical, social and spiritual—is Plutonian by nature and change at its most extreme is indicated every time Pluto is granted greatest freedom by Scorpio. This moody, passionate transit happens only once every 248.4 years—the time Pluto takes to complete its orbit around the sun—and lasts, on average, for twelve years. Just how extraordinary are these eras? Life being the testing ground for astrological assertion, past Pluto/Scorpio ages were traced by computer and cross-referenced with the course of history over the past 2,000 years. Intriguingly, this computer search of correlation revealed that some of the world's most revolutionary events transpired during Pluto/Scorpio periods, events that often precipitated a form of planetary rebirth. The findings can be summarized as follows:

Pluto/Scorpio Period	Events
A.D. 10–22	• Life and crucifixion of Christ. Traditionally, Jesus Christ is said to have died in A.D. 33, but the research of German historian Robert Eisler and Toronto astrologer William Koenig pinpoint A.D. 21 as the year of the crucifixion. Ancient records tell of Jesus' death taking place in the seventh year of Roman Emperor Tiberius, who acceded to the throne in A.D. 14. According to

Koenig, the appearance of Halley's Comet in 12 B.C. was the fabled star of Bethlehem heralding the Savior's birth.

504–515

• Rise of the Frankish empire under Clovis. Uniting many of Europe's barbarians under one ruler, the empire ranged, by A.D. 800, from the Atlantic to the Danube.

997–1008

• Widespread conversion of the Russian people to Christianity in the reign of Vladimir the Saint.
• China forcefully re-unified under the Sung dynasty—the dawn of three centuries of economic prosperity.
• Vikings land on the coast of North America.

1244–1255

• Expansion of the Mongol empire across Asia and Europe.
• Heretics hunted and burned at the stake in the first furious years of the Inquisition.
• Women's power and influence curtailed. Society succumbs to enduring ecclesiastical intimidation.

1490–1502

• The height of the Renaissance meaning, literally, "rebirth"; new learning, science, art and literature.
• The Great Age of Discovery—Christopher Columbus lands in the New World; Vasco da Gama sails to India around the Cape of Good Hope.
• Negro slavery introduced to the West Indies.

1737–1748

• The birth of the Industrial Revolution. Having its beginnings in the English textile industry, the new mechanization transformed civiliza-

tion. Work and leisure would never
be the same again.
• Massive earthquake kills 300,000
in Calcutta, India.

An Age Unprecedented

Astrologers the world over have already branded the imminent Pluto/Scorpio age as being fraught with potential more magnificent and more terrifying than history has ever known. Geological upheaval, economic collapse, nuclear war, wondrous technological innovation and the transformation of global consciousness are seen as distinct possibilities—the death of the old bringing on the birth of the new. For if Pluto has a cosmic mission it is to provoke the release of the enduring from the transitory and the outworn.

Reincarnation and karma, it must be stressed, express themselves through astrological computation—the appraisal of universal energy interacting in the physical world. Astrology is the framework of accountancy through which rebirth proceeds. Just as worlds are affected, altered and reborn by the interplay of cosmological unfoldment, so individuals are embodied in birth after birth according to the same principles. Astrology measures where we stand in the eternal order, each horoscope reflecting ancient causes. Clarice Toyne explains neatly in *Heirs to Eternity*:

> A soul is born at a certain time (as time is accounted in this our solar system) because of what he is. He is not as he is because of the star under which he was born. He is conceived and born at a certain astrological moment because the energies of his soul tune-in with the cosmic flow of star-forces at that particular time.

The same tuning-in applies, on a much grander scale, to the positioning of Pluto, Scorpio and the planet Earth. A specific pattern of energy is created by each predictable arrangement of the heavens. And this force field affects all consciousness on and within the globe—including that of rocks and minerals.

Smaller than the earth, with a diameter of 1,860 miles, Pluto has already cut inside Neptune's orbit in its slow, cyclic swing towards the sun. At perihelion in September, 1989, the planet will be 2,750 million miles from the solar furnace—hugely nearer, though hardly cheek by jowl, than its average distance of 3,667 million miles. Pluto reflects sunlight so feebly that it is only one sixteen hundredth as bright as the faintest star visible to the naked eye on a clear night. Even more occluded is the planet's moon, Charon, discovered in 1978.

God of the Underworld

The name Pluto, from the Greek *Plouton*, signifies fertility and is thought to be rooted in the Sumerian *Boro-tun*, meaning "deliverer of the womb." In ancient Greek mythology, Pluto exemplifies power and will as the unscrupulous god of the underworld. In his gloomy domain deep below ground, he receives and regenerates the souls of the dead. For Pluto ("the rich one," in Latin) is the gatekeeper of immortality and his subterranean passages are running over with the collective past of the human race. Enthroned beside his consort, Persephone, he is always invisible, a quality symbolized by his hood, made from the scalp of a dog. In keeping with this guise, Pluto's influence is veiled and usually operates subliminally for long periods before revealing itself in drastic change. Even the planet's recent discovery after untold cycles of manipulation is illustrative of the Plutonian character.

Pluto represents the unconscious—individual and collective—and governs forces buried deep in the psyches of human beings and nations. Along with many of her contemporaries, American astrologer Isabel M. Hickey maintains that the planet's obscure energy is at work behind the restlessness, chaos and confusion of the modern world. She feels that Pluto's transit through Scorpio will ensure the elimination of "ancient wrongs and evils" by touching off "a purging such as the world has never known." Although Edgar Cayce didn't express himself quite so apocalyptically, he did predict that Plutonian forces would culminate in world-wide geological upheaval by the year 1998. And he did remark (reading 1100–27) before the Second World War:

> . . . Within the next hundred to two hundred years there may be a great deal of influence (of Pluto) upon the ascendancy of man; for it's closest of those to the activities of the Earth, to be sure, and is a developing influence, not one already established.

Since these words were uttered, astrologers have elected the oncoming Pluto/Scorpio transit as the most likely time for Pluto to display, most ruthlessly, its reincarnational power. The planet could be said to be spinning towards a sort of global *bardo* state, forerunner of the much-vaunted Age of Aquarius. Laurel Lowell, a cousin of the American astronomer Percival Lowell, codiscoverer of Pluto, wrote of the years 1984–1995:

> Anguish born of regenerative forces seems to be inevitable: the so-called lower self must give way to the higher if all the adverse laws of karma are not to take effect, possibly in another incarnation—if not here and now. The soul is at stake.

British astrologer and clairvoyant John Humber sees the Pluto/Scorpio configuration demanding a leveling of global conditions. "If we haven't got things right, Pluto will let us have it," he declared. "All prejudice and unfairness will have to go and it will go either through cooperation or it will go violently. Transformation and change could come about in a beautiful way but the closer the world gets to this Pluto/Scorpio phase *without* changing, the more threatening the situation becomes." There is, however, another way of looking at this threat. "For a disease to heal, it has to break out," ventured astrologer Liz Greene in lecturing on Pluto's influence.

Pluto rules places of horror and destruction, earthquakes and volcanoes, caves, catastrophes, wars, epidemics and floods. There's the obvious link with plutonium, the synthetic radioactive element notorious for its major role in the construction of nuclear warheads. But the planet is also very much concerned with the fecundity that springs from death. In the words of astrologer Stephen Arroyo: "One of the paradoxical aspects of Pluto's nature is that its symbolism incorporates both the old life forms which are ready to be eliminated *and* the very power that will shatter these forms and effect . . . psychological-emotional surgery." Volcanic ash, for example, may suggest destruction, but it also produces the most fertile soil. Cave clay and mineral springs are found in the depths of the Earth but their properties can give new life to the sick. Archaeological discoveries, the raising of submerged treasures, cemeteries, pyramids and temples are all Plutonian. And Pluto governs interest in reincarnation, development of spiritual insight and the pineal gland, our degenerated organ of clairvoyance. Fritz Brunhübner, who wrote the first, classic work on Pluto in 1934, spoke of the planet being responsible for a reanimation and refinement of the pineal gland which would help to lead humanity "out of the mechanization and mechanical technology of our times into an epoch of revivification, of resurrection, or magic and creative power."

Like his contemporary, Edgar Cayce, Brunhübner was "thoroughly convinced" that massive Earth movements would raise the lost continent of Atlantis from the ocean floor. Rebirth of the untraceable would go hand in hand with the death of the obsolete. The influence of Pluto, he wrote, "will be transplanted to the whole international, political and economic life . . . the new spirit knocks on the door with hammer blows and dictatorially demands the reorganization and changeover."

Global Rebirth

As unwelcome as change by coercion might be, the action of Pluto, like death itself, is essential for the rebirth that evolution demands. To be reborn, first you must die! Pluto's task is to press for evolutionary perfection, to push the individual and the race through hoops of renewal in life as in death. Ideally, humanity will pursue and bring about its own rebirth by uniting in caring, understanding, and tolerance of individual differences. But, as Alexander Ruperti points out in *Cycles of Becoming*, if humans are incapable of such enlightened behaviour, then the world's population may be compelled to unite in death . . .

> Through the fire of man-made or planetary cataclysms, nuclear war or telluric upheaval, Pluto will teach people to know and feel (Scorpio) that we are all individually concerned with everything that happens to human beings everywhere on the globe.

If Pluto must invoke annihilation, it is also the turning point, the catalyst of fresh beginnings. In penetrating to the core of experience, in painfully tearing away the ephemeral from that which lasts, Pluto, the gatekeeper, is obliged to offer new horizons. Dane Rudhyar, California's grand old man of astrology, wrote that Pluto "guards the path that leads through unconscious death or conscious Crucifixion to some type of celestial re-integration." Which is all very well until we are reminded that, in this madcap nuclear age, the path over which Pluto stands sentinel is the warpath. But if Humanity is flirting with a showdown of the darkest Plutonian forces, maybe that's because, in some dim cranny of the collective unconscious, the race knows there is nothing to lose from wholesale destruction. Even the Apocalypse can take on positive overtones when seen as a flashpoint of rebirth. For exactly how the reincarnation of global consciousness is achieved matters little. From the grandest spiritual perspective, whether it is realized in the fullness of vitality or in mass extermination, the requirement is the same:

to be reborn, first you must die!

Pluto-Scorpio Transit August 27, 1984 to November 10, 1995
Global Chart Drawn and Analyzed By Astrologer Caroline Keenan

As I look at this chart, a phrase from the *Book of Changes* rises to mind: "Work on what has been spoiled" (*I Ching*, Ku 18). Karmic debt tied to ecological irresponsibility looms large in this global horoscope and a balancing of accounts is called for as Pluto transits Scorpio. In the chart, the mutable earth sign Virgo, symbolic of health, service, welfare, grains, food distribution and analysis is tenanted by:

- Sun—executive action, government, ego, image;
- Mercury—communications, transportation, news, media;
- Moon—nourishment, foodstuffs, public emotion, and
- Venus—sympathy, art, aesthetics, weather, money.

This conflicts with:

- The South Node—karmic past;
- Mars—aggression, steel, cutting edges, weapons;

- Uranus—technology, unexpected results, erratic behavior, electricity, eccentricity;
- Neptune—deception, poison, illusion, oil, synthetics, multinational corporations; and
- Jupiter—expansion, weather (especially wind), customs, power of command, unlimited growth.

These tenant the mutable fire sign Sagittarius, symbolizing flaming arrows, optimism and intellectual conceptualizing (theory). This overall positioning may bring about the following effects:

Mutation of viruses and bacteria: New York astrologer Al Morrison stated some years ago that he suspected the Pluto/Scorpio transit would bring about a mutatation of viruses and bacteria. Through indiscriminate use of pharmaceuticals, such as antibiotics, there is already evidence that certain diseases have mutated beyond the effective reach of drugs. Also, experimentation in bacterial and viral warfare, already well advanced, could get out of control.

Changing weather patterns and primordial destruction: There could be a rise in the incidence and severity of earthquakes, volcanoes, tidal waves and hurricanes which have been much in evidence since the grand transmutation of Jupiter and Saturn beginning on New Year's Eve, 1980. Misuse of technology, nuclear testing and the disturbance of ozone layers may well provoke unseasonably heavy rains, blasting winds or drought.

Problems with food distribution and production: International communication difficulties may exacerbate food shortages arising from the loss of crops through drought, pestilence or flooding.

Depletion of oil: The harvest is reaped of the human race's profligate handling of this very limited power source. Scarcity seriously curtails the world's industrial production leading to drastic unemployment and the collapse of the international money market.

War: The re-alignment of power is suggested, along with the forging of new alliances and the revival of old enmities. Ambition, greed and necessity figure strongly and could bring nuclear arms into play.

As gloomy as this exposition may sound, there is as much will to life as there is to destruction. Much has been spoiled but much can still be saved. For this to happen, however, the highest aspects of Pluto's capacity for rebirth must be exercised in a mass raising of consciousness—the world's best and bravest hope.

13

The Personal Investigation of Past Lives

Explore the River of the Soul; whence or in what order you have come . . .

ZOROASTER

Every incarnation that we remember must increase our comprehension of ourselves as we are.

ALEISTER CROWLEY

Human minds are like anchors that have lain too long on the ocean floor: to be fully appreciated, they must be lifted from the muddy deception of their working environment and scoured of clinging deposits. Just as an anchor is habitually coated with seaweed and barnacles, so the mind is beset by swarms of thought and emotion that mask its true nature. These layers of mental obscuration must be removed before the personal investigator of past lives gives the slightest consideration to actually probing for memories of earlier incarnations. Through deep meditation, attention must be withdrawn from all compelling distractions, internal as well as external, and turned over to contemplation of the eternal backdrop.

128

Then, and only then, can the mind—calm, unencumbered and receptive—be plumbed for its treasure trove of recollection.

It's not easy. The emotions of each new birth, compounded by the cares, worries and distractions of the present moment, screen the self from mind-images of former lives. That which is coarser and nearer will always blot out the finer and more remote. To surpass the consciousness of everyday living, to discard temporarily the normal way of perceiving and coping with the world, goes against all societal conditioning and requires the utmost persistence. Much like the search for gold, the trail that leads to the awakening of past-life memory usually zigzags over exacting terrain which must be negotiated tirelessly if the priceless vein, hitherto existing only at the suggestion of a stranger, is to be found and excavated. Needed all at once are the ability to relax, the power of concentration, the will to proceed and the patience to wait for results.

The technique—and there are many variations on a basic theme—is carried out without a guide or helpmate and without the aid of hypnosis. Indispensable, however, are quiet surroundings and a strong desire to cross repeatedly the chasms that separate birth from death. Yet more is required of the individual than mere desire for knowledge of past lives. Would-be explorers must have firmly decided they are willing to undertake—and ready to handle—this always unpredictable quest. Colin Bennett, the author of *Practical Time Travel*, a handbook published in 1937 to encourage the welling up of reincarnational experience, cautions the personal investigator: "Cutting adrift, however temporarily, from the particular position in time and space which we call the present moment sounds exciting, and is exciting, but is no more suitable for the spiritually unstable than is crossing the Atlantic in a fishing boat the right kind of adventure for the physically timorous." British reincarnation researcher J. H. Brennan adds: "If your doctor has warned you to avoid excitement do not turn to exploring your past lives as a soothing sedentary occupation." Assuming, however, that the adventurer feels equipped for the journey, there's nothing left to do but set out . . .

Tracking Backwards

Many names are given to the retrieval of past-life information. They range from the tantalizing "Magical Memory" of Aleister Crowley, the English mystic with the satanic reputation, to the long-winded *pubbenivasanussatinana* of Buddhism. Gautama Buddha himself, although he was said to have recalled 550 of his own past lives, didn't explain (at least, not for the record) just how he remembered his previous existences except to say that anyone who wished to do likewise "must be perfect in the precepts, bring his emotions to a state of quiescence, practice the trances diligently, attain to illumination, and dwell in solitude." Buddha laid great stress on determination to succeed because "if the mind be fixed on the acquirement of any object, that object will be attained." A devotee, he said, should say to himself:

> Let me call to mind many previous states of existence, as, one birth, two births . . . twenty births . . . one hundred births, one thousand births, one hundred thousand births . . . saying: I lived in such a place, had such a name . . . Then I passed from that existence, and was reborn in such a place. There also I had such a name, was of such a family, of such a caste, had such possessions, experienced such joys and sorrows, and such a length of life. Then I passed from that existence and was reborn in this existence. Thus let me call to mind many former states of existence, and let me precisely define them.

Buddhaghosha, a sage whose name means the Voice of Buddha, gave more explicit instructions as to how past lives could be retrieved. In a passage from the *Vishuddhi Marga* or *Path of Purity* he advises fellow Buddhists to meditate deeply on events which have just taken place, and then to recall them in reverse succession. Absorbed in after-breakfast meditation, when he has returned from collecting alms, the devotee should

. . . consider the event which last took place, namely, his sitting down; next the spreading of the mat; the entering of the room; the putting away of bowl and robe; his eating; his leaving the village; his going the rounds of the village for alms; his entering the village. . . . Thus must he consider all that he did for a whole day and night, going backwards over it in reverse order.

Once a full day's remembrance has been achieved without any gaps or obscure episodes, says Buddhaghosha, the devotee should push back his memory—still in reverse order—to the day before, and the day before that, ten days before, a month, a year, ten years, twenty years, and so on. Any broken links in the chain of memory must be repaired by plunging back into the trance of association. When memory has been revived uninterruptedly as far back as conception, the supreme challenge is to harness sufficient intensity of concentration to penetrate even further to a name and form at the moment of death in the previous life. Buddhaghosha is sympathetic to the extreme arduousness of this test, recognizing that "this point of time is like thick darkness and difficult to be made out by the mind of any person still deluded." Nevertheless, he urges a nondespairing outlook, calling upon the student to repeatedly fix his mind on the void which "in no long time" will yield the desired knowledge. Once the previous existence has been retrieved, other existences will be easier to call to mind, says Buddhaghosha. In his book *A Hermit in the Himalayas*, Paul Brunton writes that the learned monk who instructed him in Buddhism had practised these meditations for twenty years and could testify to their effectiveness. But the monk also admitted that few Buddhists were able to pursue the method with success as the concentration and effort required were so fearfully difficult and prolonged.

Yoga has been defined as "the cessation of agitation of the consciousness" and is, accordingly, a perfect vehicle for the generation of past-life memory. Ironically, Hindu belief in reincarnation is one reason why many natives of India shun yogic practices. Firmly assured of future lives, they consciously postpone personal striving for perfection to another lifetime! But that neither negates nor alters the aim of yoga (stemming from the Sanskrit word *yuj* meaning union), which is to awaken cosmic consciousness at the earliest opportunity and so to leap clear of the dreaded wheel of rebirth. Remembering past lives is part of the overall process. The indeterminably ancient sutras of Patanjali, the earliest yogic texts, point out that all experience of previous births remains in *chitta*, that is, in the subconscious mind. This experience can be recovered at will by the advanced spiritual aspirant through *samyama*, or the rapt absorption of thought waves. Patanjali wrote: "Concentrate on the impressions of the past; know past lives."

Rudolf Steiner said the same thing in a different way when he replied, "The entrance to the path is opened by right meditation" in answer to those curious to know why people do not normally remember past lives. More explicitly, Steiner recommended that those wishing to recover memories of pre-existence enlist the help of an imaginary detachable double every time something seems to happen by chance. Suppose a tile falls from a roof and injures a person's shoulders. Rather than blame this injury on bad luck, the person should visualize an imaginary man or woman who climbs onto the roof in question, loosens a tile and quickly returns to ground level so that the dislodged tile may fall on his/her shoulders. Steiner said that this exercise of seeing ourselves deliberately bringing about events that may appear to happen by accident "can ultimately promote in every human being a kind of certainty of having existed in an earlier life—certainty through having engendered a feeling of inner impressions which he knows were most definitely not received in this life."

For Aleister Crowley, a frequent dam in the river of past-life memory was the suppression of painful episodes, primarily death experiences, by the subconscious. "One instinctively flinches from remembering one's last, as one does from imagining one's next, death," he wrote. But if the "tricks of the trade"were practised diligently, even "Freudian forgetfulness" could be conquered so as to liberate the full flood of Magical Memory. Crowley's backward-looking past-life exercises bear more than a passing resemblance to the Buddhist technique expounded some 2,500 years earlier. First of all, he urged would-be adepts to learn to write backwards with either hand, to walk backwards, to speak backwards ("Eh ma I" instead of "I am He"), and to read backwards. He then invoked the Buddhaghosha method of recalling events in reverse order. A regression of five minutes must be perfected before extending the backward run to a day and, eventually, a lifetime. (Says Crowley: "The extension from a day to the course of his whole life will not prove so difficult as the perfecting of the five minutes.") Practice, which in time becomes almost mechanical, should be carried out at least four times a day. Only when the mind has been allowed to return one hundred times to the hour of birth should it be encouraged to run back even further—and that's when the Magical Memory, with any luck, starts to unfold. Crowley cautions all to cross-check with historical and geographical fact the contents of these apparently preincarnate recollections, "always reflecting upon the fallibility even of such safeguards." But there's another test for the real thing. He writes in *Magick in Theory and Practice*:

> Genuine recollections almost invariably explain oneself to oneself. Suppose, for example, that you feel an instinctive aversion to some particular kind of wine. Try as you will, you can find no reason for your idiosyncracy. Suppose, then, that when you explore some previous incarnation, you remember that you died by a poison administered in a wine of that character, your aversion is explained by the proverb: "A burnt child dreads the fire."

And there are other intimations of authenticity. Crowley again:

> There is a sense which assures us intuitively when we are running on a scent breast high. There is an *oddness* about the memory which is somehow annoying. It gives a feeling of shame and guiltiness. There is a tendency to blush. One feels like a schoolboy caught red-handed in the act of writing poetry. There is the same sort of feeling as one has when one finds a faded photograph or a lock of hair twenty years old among the rubbish in some forgotten cabi-

net. This feeling is independent of the question whether the thing remembered was in itself a source of pleasure or of pain. Can it be that we resent the idea of our "previous condition of servitude"? We want to forget the past, however good reason we may have to be proud of it. It is well known that many men are embarrassed in the presence of a monkey.

When the personal investigator does not experience this self-consciousness—expressed more forcefully by Colin Bennett as self-disgust—the accuracy of the memory is more open to question than usual. Distrust, as well as rigorous historical enquiry, should be directed towards any glamorous past life that emerges. And distrust should turn to outright skepticism if results indicate the investigator is the reincarnation of a famous person. As conceivable as a past life of historical renown might be, it is much more likely to be the product of overblown fantasy, self-deception being an ever-present danger in every occult area of inquiry. The groundbreaking work of responsible reincarnation researchers can only be undermined by the myriad claims of those convinced they once were Napoleon, Julius Caesar, Henry VIII, Cleopatra, Joan of Arc and others. Enough is enough.

Gazing into the Past

Mercifully, the act of sustained mental retrogression is not the only way to contact past lives without undergoing hypnosis. There's a technique for visualizing a clock face in order to "think away" the dial and bring on a trance state that carries the investigator back through time and space. Not so difficult as back-pedaling the memory to past lives, the following exercise still makes huge demands:

To begin, select a clock face which can be watched quietly and without interruption. Note the size of the face and every single detail that it encloses—the outline of the numerals, the shape of the hands, the manufacturer's name, the layout and ornamenta-

*tion. Concentrate on assimilating a complete picture
of the clock face and, after five minutes, close your
eyes and try to recall precisely what you have been
looking at.*

*Only when the dial has been reproduced in the
mind's eye with perfect clarity should the disman-
tling process begin. First, imagine the minute hand
has been removed so that the dial is complete in
every detail but for its single-handedness. Next, "think
away" the hour hand; then remove the ornamenta-
tion and the maker's name. Acutely aware that time
itself is being thought into nonexistence, you similarly despatch the numerals. You are now confronted
with a blank clock face which must be seen to become smaller and smaller until it disappears completely. All the while, you are thinking: "Time is
flowing backwards." Now all that remains is the
clock's support. When this has been imagined into
extinction the last link with time has been removed
and the resulting trance state carries you back into
another life . . .*

As uncomplicated as this method may sound, immediate
success is highly improbable. A few weeks of diligent practice
can bring results to the willful and the perservering, but
there are those who proceed with this exercise in vain.

By gazing intently into a crystal ball or goldfish bowl
filled with water, a road of living memory can be thought into
existence, a road leading from the self into the deepest heart
of the crystal. Tibetans employ this method with black crystalline stones found in mountain streams while, in India,
natives use a small bowl or saucer—or even cupped hands—
filled with ink. Once a strong psychic link has been established between the investigator and the object of concentration,
time slowly recedes, rolling backwards through the present
life before leaping into past incarnations. The procedure has
an inbuilt speed of its own and will not be hurried. Initially,
no more than twenty minutes or half an hour should be spent
on this exercise, to be repeated not more than once a day
until results become decisive. Writes Colin Bennett: "The
earliest superphysical phenomenon is often a clouding of the

crystal's surface with thin blue haze which may extend above the sphere and hover over it like a patch of mist. Once this appearance is seen it is only a matter of patience before the cloud in front of the crystal's face parts or disperses giving place to a picture."

Alternatively, an archetypal symbol can be used as the object of concentration—a symbol such as an eye, circle, sun, cross, triangle or, perhaps, one of the numbers from one to ten. Acting as a mind-sensitizer, the chosen symbol (visualization can be aided by a drawing) will become a channel for the drawing of energy from the deep unconscious and the inner eye will be swept by flashes of scenes from past lives. Each passing fragment constitutes a potential clue and the investigator is advised to jot down each one in the hope that a pattern will emerge of one or more former lives.

The annotation and analysis of dreams can also awaken deep memory. The individual's dream records tend to hover around a few central thoughts and incidents—pointers to deeply felt experiences of the past which have contributed greatly to the character and personality of the present. To dream is to travel beyond time, and to travel beyond time is to swirl through a maelstrom of hints and impressions that may reveal who we are, where we've been and where we're going. Making sense of this fourth-dimensional bombardment is another matter altogether. Colin Bennett recommends that prolonged study of personal dream records be followed by lying back, closing the eyes, relaxing all muscles and allowing the mind to become as blank as possible. "Out of the resulting state of semiconsciousness," he says, "the sought-for truth appears as though it were an incident acted upon a stage, or seen in a moving picture."

The worldwide Rosicrucian Order, with 250,000 members in more than 180 countries, has preserved and developed more than eighty different types of exercises for the restoration of past-life memory. The underlying motive of these mental work-outs is that of the Rosicrucian movement itself—to awaken cosmic consciousness in the individual. Taking various approaches to meditation and guided visualization, the exercises are directed at answering the question: How can I be more effective, more creative and more whole today? Rosicrucians stress that the value of the reincarnational experience is determined by its usefulness during this life-time. "The most important point to remember," notes the *Rosicrucian Digest* of October 1979, "is that at the individual level, reincarnation becomes not a question of proof or faith but of personal *experiences* that give meaning and dimension to our present life."

Seers and occultists have long talked about the Akashic Records as the indelible impressions left upon the etheric substance of the universe by everything that has ever happened. In a lecture given in 1931, Edgar Cayce described a typical out-of-body journey which gave him access to this warehouse in the sky. "I entered this temple and found in it a very large room, very much like a library," he said. "Here were the books of people's lives, for each person's activities were a matter of actual record, it seemed. And I merely had to pull down the record of the individual for whom I was seeking information." Far from being the sole preserve of great mystics, these Akashic Records—which Cayce said were "to the mental world as the cinema is to the physical world" —are open for inspection by anyone who is able to travel to the astral plane. J. H. Brennan says that by an act of imagination it is possible for the individual to create an astral shell capable of interacting with the Akashic Records. He suggests flexing the imagination with a walk towards Cayce's library, visualizing the scene for no more than ten minutes daily for the first two weeks and thereafter—at least until complete identification is achieved—for no longer than fifteen minutes. The investigator's patience will be sorely tried as he is asked to do the following:

(a) *For the first week, after relaxing the mind with closed eyes, visualize walking down a corridor towards a door. Clarify and add to the picture each day until the corridor takes on absolute familiarity.*

(b) *No earlier than a week later—when the corridor is as vivid as it can possibly be—picture opening the door and entering a massive library. Spend at least two weeks, preferably longer, building up minute details of this library. Note the multitude of sections, the billions of volumes on the*

      shelves, the vast space involved. For in this col-
      lection is recorded every detail on every person
      who has ever lived.

(c) *Attempt no short cuts—they will only ruin the*
      project. Every possible detail must be assimi-
      lated before the vision is complete. When this
      happens, keep building and reexamining the pic-
      ture for another week. Then walk to the section
      of the library which houses your life history and
      search the shelves for the volume that bears
      your name. Withdraw the book and read your
      reincarnational history. Before acceptance, cross-
      check all the resulting information—some of it
      visualized, some arising in picture-image form—
      with known facts.

Akashic exploration may not always be so straightforward. Occultist Alice Bailey warned that fleeting glimpses of
the Akashic film don't necessarily pertain to the viewer as
much as the viewer would like to think they do. "This is not
the case," she wrote, "any more than the people and activities seen out of any window in a big city reveal to the
onlooker his own relatives, friends and pursuits." Certainly,
only the most vigorous visualization can bring results. And
even these results are suspect until proven sound.

The Christos Experience

Retaining visualization as the primary technique, it *is*
possible—some would say preferable—to explore past lives
with the help of others. The Christos Experience, in which a
person's ankles and "third eye" area are massaged simultaneously to induce lucid, conscious "dreaming," has carried its
subjects into the wildest terrain for the most exotic experiences. Writer Gerry Glaskin, who has championed the technique which he found in an obscure West Australian magazine
in 1971, confessed to being "shattered" by his first Christos
voyage. He wrote in *A Door to Eternity*:

      Prior to this experience . . . I had not even consid-
      ered, let alone been convinced of, the possibility of

previous lives or reincarnation. My religious up-
bringing had denied it completely. But now, nevertheless, I could clearly see "myself" with dark skin,
long thin limbs and a body well over six feet tall,
with long and very different features to myself—a
man, moreover, in his thirties, instead of almost
fifty as I was then. "I" was dressed in a garment and
headband that I could only conjecture to be Egyptian . . .

In another Christos journey, Glaskin saw himself as a
primitive being on the run from other savages. One woman
experimenter described being in the body of an albatross
gliding over cold southern oceans. And, as if to show the
method can conjure up future visions too, a man who had
described a small village surrounded by mountains later returned from his honeymoon in Norway to reveal that he had
visited the exact scene encountered during his Christos experience! Here's an abbreviated description of the technique:

(a) *The subject, who must be relaxed, is to lie,
shoeless, on the floor with a cushion under his
head. One helper massages the subject's ankles
for two to three minutes to aid relaxation. The
other—usually the Christos "guide"—massages
the "third eye" position, that is, the lower centre
of the forehead. This massaging is done vigorously with the edge of the curved hand and
should continue until the subject's head is buzzing.*

(b) *Ask the subject—who is now encouraged to talk
so that he will later feel at ease in describing the
experience—to visualize himself growing 2 inches
longer through the bottoms of his feet. Once the
subject has stretched, ask him to return his feet
to their normal position. The process is repeated,
but this time the subject is asked to grow longer
through his head. Return to the feet, asking the
subject to visualize a 12-inch stretch. Repeat the
process through the head—and return. Back to
the feet for a 24-inch stretch. This time the
subject must hold the stretch while extending the*

same distance through the head. Once extended 4 feet, he should feel himself expanding, like a balloon.

(c) Ask the subject to use his expanded consciousness to describe fully his own front door and its surroundings—including what he is standing on and what is above him when he looks up. Next, ask him to imagine he is standing on top of his roof and to describe the scene below. Now tell him to rise about 500 yards and to keep describing all he sees. He should turn slowly, in a complete circle, relating all. Ask him what time it is and elicit a description of the weather conditions. Get him to change the scene from day to night and back to day again and ask him to compare both scenes. Next—to give him an assurance of safety—ask who is changing daylight to darkness. It is very important that he realizes he has control over whatever he sees.

(d) Now for the experience which could yield a past life. Tell the subject to keep the picture in bright sunlight so that he can see where he lands. Ask him for a description of his feet (bare or with shoes?), the ground he is standing on, the people and events around him, his clothes, his features, etc. Keep pressing for more and more details. Watch the eyelids for rapid eye and eye-muscle movements—the faster the flicker, the more successful are the subject's visions. Follow up his answers with pertinent questions. Let the visit take its course until the subject wishes to return to the present. He is not in a trance and should, if asked, be able to identify local sounds while experiencing the events of a different time frame. Although the full procedure is likely to take an hour or more, the subject will probably think he has been traveling for only a quarter of the time.

Visualization is given another twist by Bryan Jameison's "montage time-lap" method in which imaginary light switches, placed strategically on the body, are turned off one by one before a make-believe elevator carries the subject to the threshold of a past-life experience. The average, first-time subject takes only eight minutes to reach an altered state of consciousness. "Doing a time-lap regression is amazingly easy," writes Jameison. "It doesn't involve the use of drugs, a deep hypnotic trance, arduous meditation, hocus-pocus or any mysterious rite . . . It's as easy as playing tic-tac-toe." Devised for subject and guide, the method goes like this:

(a) *Choose a very dimly lit room without any distractions. Ask the subject to lie down and take five deep breaths with eyes closed.*

(b) *Instruct the subject to visualize common wall light switches at the key body points and to turn them off in the following order: right foot, right knee, right hip, left foot, left knee, left hip, back of right hand, right elbow, right shoulder, back of left hand, left elbow, left shoulder, top of the head, mid-forehead, throat, base of the spine, back of the neck.*

(c) *Once the subject has visualized an elevator, ask him to approach it, push the call button and, on its arrival, to step inside and face the front. Guided by his superconscious, he should then select a floor most conducive to the reliving of a past life and describe what he sees when the elevator stops and the doors open. (*SPECIAL NOTE: *If the subject sees a life scene on leaving the elevator, ask him to check whether he's in a former body. If clouds are seen instead of a hallway, ask him to move into the clouds and go back in time to the first important earth life. Should this happen, disregard the next step.)*

(d) *If the subject sees a hallway or tunnel, ask him to move to the end of the passage, describing his progress. Then ask him to locate and move through a door leading from the passageway and to report what he sees on the other side. If he's confronted with a scene from a past life, check to see whether he's in a body. This being so, he*

> *should breathe deeply and relax in his new
> surroundings.*
>
> (e) *Question the subject as to identity, age, race
> and ability to use his senses. Ask him to go back
> in time to the age of fifteen and move him slowly
> through that life, hitting as many major events
> as possible. Allow him to experience death and
> to review the life as a whole. Inquire about the
> possibility of people prominent in that life hav-
> ing bearing on the present existence.* (NOTE:
> *Should the subject start to relive a particularly
> exciting or traumatic episode, he will begin
> breathing heavily. If this happens, ask him to
> leave the body temporarily or move him forward
> to a more peaceful period.)*
>
> (f) *Invite the subject to return to the first Earth life
> relevant to that of today and repeat the life-
> death cycle. Bring him forward in stages of
> twenty-five, fifty or one hundred years, grant-
> ing the opportunity of experiencing as many lives
> as possible. The subject can return to the pres-
> ent moment whenever he wishes—simply ask him
> to take a deep breath and open his eyes. To
> reduce the risk of headache, ensure that he re-
> mains still for a few minutes at the close of the
> regression.*

As overwhelming as intellectual conviction might be, nothing convinces quite like the emotional jolt of personal experience. That's why the investigation of past lives is worth pursuing: the plausible stands to be transformed into the tangible, unifying the head with the heart. The finest results, however, cannot be won through mere technique. A new way of being is called for in which the horizons of perception are rolled back in all directions. In *The Memory of Past Births*, Charles Johnston, a retired member of the Bengal Civil Service, wrote in 1899 ". . . it is only in proportion as we inherit our immortality, and consciously rise above the barriers of time, that we can possibly inherit the memory of our past." A past, moreover, that can help dissolve some of the perplexity of the present, for everything that we are has its roots in bygone incarnations. Unconsciously, we are the aggregate of all our lives. In striving to make the unconscious conscious, in demanding to *know*, lies the thrill and the reward of the personal investigation of past-life memory. At times, the evidence may be hard to come by and even harder to interpret. But, in the words of Aleister Crowley: "Anything which throws light upon the Universe, anything which reveals us to ourselves, should be welcome in this world of riddles."

14

From The Dalai Lama to the Population Conundrum

The nature of the case for reincarnation is multifaceted and multidimensional, often quixotic yet essentially changeless. Here, before the evidence is summarized, are some further perspectives on rebirth seen from a variety of windows.

Reincarnation Personified

The fourteenth Dalai Lama, self-exiled ruler of 6,000,000 Tibetans, is the most famous personification of rebirth in the world today. Each Dalai Lama (a Mongolian expression meaning "greatest teacher") is understood to be not only his predecessor reborn but also the reincarnation of the entire line of Tibetan god-kings traceable to the year 1391. Whenever a Dalai Lama dies, an exhaustive search is mounted for the infant reincarnation of the dead leader who, as the embodiment of *Chenrizeg*, the Buddhist god of grace, is considered to rush back to earth in order to help the human race. Far from being a masquerade orchestrated by Tibetan king-makers to placate a public with metaphysical inclinations, the search incorporates stringent recognition tests not unlike those employed by Western reincarnation researchers. While lesser candidates are easily disqualified by these trials, eyewitnesses have testified to the remarkable responses they elicit from the real Dalai Lama.

The present Dalai Lama, whose personal name is Tenzin Gyatso, was born on June 6, 1935. He was found after the search groups had fanned out eastwards from Lhasa, the Tibetan capital, in response to mystical hints that the new ruler was to be found in the direction of the rising sun. First of all, the head of the late Dalai Lama (who sat in state after his death in 1933) was found mysteriously turned to the East from the traditional southerly position. When the state oracle was consulted about this development, the monk seer, deep in trance, flung a white scarf in an easterly direction. Praying incessantly for further guidance, the Tibetan regent went on a pilgrimage to the lake of Chos Khorgyal, as all who peer into its depths are said to be able to see something of the future. The regent's gaze was met by a vision of a three-storeyed temple with a turquoise roof standing close to a house with carved gables and blue eaves. Details of the vision were written down and kept secret by the search parties which, in 1937, set out to look for the infant king in much the same fashion as the wise men of the East had ventured in search of the baby Jesus. Tibetans at large, knowing the recovery of their monarch was vital to the national interest, were eager for news of the mission's progress. To be without the Dalai Lama was to be an orphan nation.

One search group, disheartened after months of arduous and fruitless wandering on horseback, had penetrated deep into Chinese territory. In their panniers were objects that had belonged to the thirteenth Dalai Lama. Although several boys had been questioned along the way regarding these objects, none had come close enough in their answers to meet divine requirements. But as they entered the village of Takster in the Chinese province of Chinghai, the searchers' spirits revived dramatically at the sight of a three-storeyed temple standing not far from a family dwelling. The scene was just as the vision had described. Excitedly, the leader of the party exchanged clothes with a servant, a customary ploy during these all-important searches so that the royal inquiry could proceed in humble places without attracting unwanted attention. Entering the kitchen of the "house of the blue-coloured eaves," the leader was greeted by a two-year-old who demanded the rosary draped around his neck. The rosary had belonged to the thirteenth Dalai Lama and the disguised leader promised to hand it over if the boy could tell him who he was. The child replied *"Seraga"* which, in the local dialect, means "a lama of Lhasa's Sera monastery." The boy proceeded to name correctly each member of the search party. And, from an assortment of articles gathered to mislead, he identified, without the least self-consciousness, more rosaries, a drum and a walking stick that had belonged to the previous Dalai Lama. Furthermore, the boy's body was found to bear all the marks of a true incarnation of *Chenrizeg*— large, noticeable ears and moles placed on his trunk in precise accordance with tradition. The boy's parents turned out to be pure Tibetan, even though they lived in an area that had been annexed by China for twenty-seven years. Satisfied they had located the reborn Dalai Lama, the party arranged for the future ruler of Tibet to be escorted back to Lhasa. The journey, however, could not be undertaken before the searchers agreed to pay the blackmailing provincial governor 300,000 Chinese yuan (roughly $300,000) for their precious charge.

When the Chinese invaded Tibet in 1959, The Dalai Lama fled to India with many other Tibetans. He is still based there today, with headquarters at Dharamsala in the Himalayas, but spends much time visiting other Buddhist countries as well as Western nations. In his memoirs *My Land and My People*, The Dalai Lama summed up his understanding of the rebirth principle:

> The immediate source of a body is that of its parents. But physical matter cannot produce mind, nor mind matter. The immediate source of a mind must, therefore, be a mind which existed before the conception took place; the mind must have a continuity from a previous mind. This we hold to prove the existence of a past life.

Although The Dalai Lama has only the haziest of recollections of being discovered by the royal search party back in 1937, he does remember recognizing people and places known in Lhasa by his predecessor. And he chooses to interpret the continued oppression of Tibet by its Chinese conquerors in terms of national karma engendered in another age. "The aggression must have come because we did something bad," the Dalai Lama told *The New York Times* in November 1967.

Coming Back Alike

Successive incarnations, it is contended, can bear great physical resemblance to one another. Joseph Myers, a parapsychologist and consulting engineer of Lexington, North Carolina, declares: "One's personal appearance shouldn't alter from one life to the next any more than a man's appearance will be altered by age during one lifetime." Myers is convinced he was Edward Bellamy, the nineteenth-century writer of utopian novels. He even claims to remember writing these works and says he recalls most vividly the author's agonizing death from tuberculosis.

Encouraging the flow of reincarnational memory and psychic intuition by prolonged daily meditation, Myers has since claimed that Walt Disney was Charles Dickens reborn, that Mario Lanza was Caruso, that George Bernard Shaw was Voltaire, that Danny Kaye has sprung from Hans Christian Andersen. As similar as illustrations of these and other celebrated pairings are seen to be, Myers' like-begets-like hypothesis is by no means incontestable. Its fascination is that it brings a new dimension to the widely accepted assertion that predominant traits are carried over from life to life.

English mystic Clarice Toyne makes the same case as Myers in her book *Heirs to Eternity*. Besides binding G. K. Chesterton to Samuel Johnson and Sir Winston Churchill to Thomas Wentworth, she, too, pairs off Shaw and Voltaire, Kaye and Andersen, pointing out that the linking of names comes to her, spoken clearly, while she's preoccupied with chores or while walking her dogs. On researching the lives and likenesses of the suggested subjects she would "thrill to find the same bone formation of head, the same physiognomy, the same subtlety of countenance." Clarice Toyne here explains the uncanny resemblance of apparently consecutive incarnations:

Always there is a comparable overall energy-charge
which *is* the inner being, which enters and sustains
the new form. The ladder of natural evolution is
gradual and slight in its changes, not sudden and
startling in differences of form and mental calibre.
So, a returning soul has features similar to his or her
last lineaments even when there is a change of race.

In 1946, long before Clarice Toyne and Joseph Myers
had voiced their claims for reincarnational look-alikes, Harold
W. Percival maintained in his 1,000-page metaphysical trea-
tise *Thinking and Destiny* that photographs taken of the
average individual at corresponding periods in two or more
lives would show little change. The features furnished by
heredity—no matter who the parents may be—are the same
for a string of lives, Percival believed.

Reincarnation researchers have sometimes attested to
physical likeness shared between their subjects and claimed
previous personalties. The case of Sinha Oliviero, daughter of
a prosperous Brazilian rancher, is typical in that people knowing both Sinha and Marta Lorens, who professed to remember living as Sinha, were impressed by similarities in their
appearance and handwriting. Sinha died of tuberculosis at the
age of twenty-eight in October, 1917, having promised her
friend Ida Lorens, the wife of the local schoolteacher, that
she would return as her daughter. Ten months later, Marta
Lorens was born and—at the age of two and a half years—
began to speak volubly about Sinha's life.

Life Readings of the Sleeping Propet

Edgar Cayce, the greatest American clairvoyant of the
twentieth century, didn't believe a word he was saying. The
date was August 10, 1923, and Cayce, deep in a self-imposed
hypnotic trance, was asserting—contrary to his conscious
belief—that people are reborn in different bodies. Listening
subsequently to a transcript of his words, Cayce was shocked
and confounded. For reincarnation was alien and repulsive to
the sensibilities of this devout Presbyterian who taught a
Sunday school class and read the Bible daily.

Arthur Lammers, the well-to-do printer who had paid Cayce's expenses from Selma, Alabama, so that he could question him on reincarnation, was as delighted as the famous seer of Virginia Beach was dismayed and disillusioned. The answers given by the "sleeping prophet," as Cayce was known, were all Lammers needed to confirm his already well-developed fascination with rebirth, the occult and Eastern religions. Although initially fearful that his subconscious faculties had been commandeered by the devil, Cayce gradually came to accept reincarnation, realizing that it did not impugn the teachings of Jesus Christ. In time, he saw Jesus as an advanced adept who had materialized in twenty-nine previous incarnations.

While using his trance powers principally for healing, Edgar Cayce gave 2,500 "life" readings over the next twenty-one years. Drawing on the Akashic Records and the individual's unconscious mind, he described personal histories spanning many incarnations. The readings pointed strongly to the recurrent grouping of souls on Earth and detected "karmic patterns," often tracing present infirmity to deeds—or lack of deeds—in past lives. Cayce believed each soul has subconscious access to characteristics and skills accumulated in previous lives while also being subject to the influence of lives ruled by negative emotions such as hate and fear. The sleeping prophet was bluntness itself. He once told a deaf person: "Then do not close your ears again to those who plead for aid." And a sufferer of tuberculosis of the spine was greeted with: "The entity thwarted others and is meeting it now in himself." Again and again, in readings given for children suffering from all kinds of afflictions, Cayce would say: "This is karma, for both the parent and the child." The conventional conception of heredity was denied outright. When someone asked: "From which side of my family do I inherit most?" Cayce retorted: "You have inherited most from yourself, not from your family! The family is only a river through which the soul flows."

According to Cayce, the rapacious Conquistadors who stormed across Latin America in the sixteenth century suffered for their slaughter and plunder by reincarnating collectively in Spain in modern times. The cruelty they had unleashed against the Aztecs and the Incas they vented against themselves retributively during the Spanish Civil War. Similarly, those who participated in the destruction of Atlantis are now said to be on Earth in large numbers. Cayce declared:

> Granting that reincarnation is a fact, and that souls once occupied such an environ as Atlantis, and that these are now entering the Earth's sphere—if they made such alterations in the Earth's affairs in their day as to bring destruction on themselves—can there by any wonder that they might make such like changes in the affairs of peoples and individuals today?

Few of the life readings—almost half of which trace a person's reincarnational history back to Atlantis—give data that can be verified and many, suspiciously, are linked with the lives of famous people. Jesus Christ (a number of children had been "blessed by Him"), Nero, Reubens and Captain Kidd, as well as a courtyard full of priestesses and regal personages, figure in the readings which show very little change of sex in successive incarnations. For all this, some readings were nothing short of astounding. In *Many Mansions*, Gina Cerminara tells how one of Cayce's visitors was informed he had been Barnett Seay, a Southern soldier in the Civil War, in his former life. He was told further that he had lived in Henrico County, Virginia, and that records pertaining to this former personality still existed. Eagerly, the man set off for Henrico County to be redirected to the Virginia State Historical Library where many old registries had been relocated. Pursuing the scent to the library's archives, he found a record of Barnett A. Seay who had enlisted in General Lee's army as a color-bearer in 1862, at the age of twenty-one.

Cayce himself was said to have been last born in 1742 as John Bainbridge, an adventurer who ranged from Florida to the Canadian border involving himself in skirmishes with Indian tribes. But he also recalled other incarnations—including one as a priest named Ra-Ta who lived in ancient Egypt. He's on record as predicting that he will return to Earth in 1998, possibly as "a liberator of the world."

Xenoglossy

People who speak spontaneously in an unknown, perhaps extinct, foreign language are compelling witnesses for the reincarnation hypothesis. This rare, involuntary talent is known as xenoglossy—a term coined by the Nobel prize winning French physiologist and psychical researcher Dr. Charles Richet—and stems from the Greek *xeno*, meaning strange or foreign, and *glossa*, meaning tongue. Never lacking in dramatic impact, xenoglossy suggests the outpouring of subconscious memory.

In a case reported in the *Journal of the American Society for Psychical Research* (July, 1980), Dr. Ian Stevenson and Dr. Satwant Pasricha argue that Uttara Huddar, a single woman living in west central India who suddenly changed personality and started speaking nineteenth-century Bengali, was most probably giving vent to memories of a former life. Uttara, whose native tongue is Marathi, was thirty-two years of age when, in 1974, she became Sharada, a shy, married woman with a taste for Bengali clothes, food and devotional songs. Uttara and her family had to communicate with gestures until speakers of Bengali could be located.

While Sharada was poorly educated and subservient, as might be expected of a housewife of West Bengal in the early 1800s, Uttara is outgoing and highly educated, having obtained a master's degree in English and public administration. Uttara couldn't remember what took place during her times as Sharada who was utterly lost in the modern world, being a stranger to cars, trains and modern appliances as well as Uttara's locality and family to whom she referred in Bengali as "these people." Furthermore, Sharada, whose appearances lasted for days or weeks at a time, seemed unaware of anything that followed a snake bite on the toe which appeared to have ended her life at the age of twenty-two. Sharada's linguistic style (her ability to carry out conversations in Bengali is defined as "responsive xenoglossy") was devoid of all modern terms which have crept into the language since the industrial revolution. The researchers established that there was very little chance that Uttara could have inherited or acquired through normal channels her sudden, fluent knowledge of Bengali. And they found genealogical records bearing the names of a family corresponding to information given by Sharada. An 1827 property agreement between relatives named by Sharada was brought to light.

Although possession by a discarnate entity cannot be ruled out, much of the evidence points to the persistence of past-life memory. Uttara had a phobia about snakes as a child and her mother suffered nightmares, when pregnant with Uttara, of being bitten on the toe by a snake. In summing up the case, Stevenson and Pasricha declare: "We cannot say how Uttara obtained these memories of a previous life; but the feature of responsive xenoglossy tells strongly against the interpretation that she acquired them by extrasensory perception. We are, therefore, entitled to conjecture, at least provisionally, that Sharada was a previous incarnation of the person now identifed as Uttara."

Back in November, 1930, the *New York Evening Post* reported that a four-year-old girl living in Warsaw was able to speak Gaelic even though her parents conversed only in Polish. More recently, the popularity of hypnotic regression has encouraged a greater incidence of xenoglossy. Normally English-speaking Californians have surprised themselves by talking in all kinds of languages, including jungle dialects, while lying on Dr. Morris Netherton's couch. Most extraordinary of all was the case of a blond, blue-eyed eleven-year-old boy who was taped for eleven minutes as he spoke in a Chinese dialect. The tape was taken to an elderly Chinese professor at the Department of Oriental Studies, University of California, who confirmed, much to his amazement, that the boy was reciting a text from a forbidden religion of ancient China. "With some people," says Netherton, "there is no language at all. All I get are grunts and groans and I get them to translate." Thorwald Dethlefsen reports that, while conducting a regression in German, he can usually extract certain answers in the "original language." But some hypnotherapists would rather avoid altogether xenoglossy's confusing exoticism. Dr. Edith Fiore writes that ". . . just to be on the safe side, before regressing subjects I suggest that they will respond to me in English."

One of the finest and most carefully studied examples of xenoglossy was uncovered by Dr. Joel Whitton of Toronto whose anonymous subject—a psychologist with a "responsible position in the assessment and treatment of children with learning and behavioral disorders"—remembered under hypnosis two ancient languages that, presumably, he had spoken during previous incarnations. The first language was Norsk, the precursor of modern Icelandic. In deep trance, he remembered a life as a raiding warrior in a small Viking army about the year A.D. 1000 and heard the voice of Thor, his assumed previous personality, respond to questions about his ship and life at sea. He then wrote down a phonetic rendering of these responses which were later examined independently by specialists fluent in Icelandic and Norwegian. Several words and phrases were identified, most of them relating to the sea and ships.

The psychologist also described living as a young man in Mesopotamia (part of Persia) in A.D. 625 and proceeded to write in the language of the day. (This, strictly speaking, is xenography rather than xenoglossy.) Samples of his spidery, childlike script were verified by Dr. Idrahim Pourhadi of the Near East Section of Washington's Library of Congress as being *Sassanid Pahlavi*—a form of writing that has not been used since A.D. 651 and bears no relation to present-day Iranian.

An Ailment Relieved

As Canada's only university professor lecturing on the empirical evidence for reincarnation, Ian Currie adopted a purely academic approach to his subject—but he had reckoned without past-life reprisals! After writing *You Cannot Die*, a best-selling documentation of immortality, Currie developed a personal ailment which left him in nagging discomfort at the height of the book's American promotion during the summer of 1979. For the next three years, doctors could do nothing for him, attributing the physical symptoms to psychological causes. And this, in turn, set Currie wondering about the hidden influence of past lives. So he approached Toronto's Dr. Joel Whitton, psychiatrist, neurophysiologist and past-life therapist, in the hope of ridding himself of the troublesome symptom.

Regular weekly hypnotherapy sessions with Whitton enabled Currie to tap seven past-life personalities ranging from a builder in ancient Egypt to a seventeenth-century nun in the Low Countries before making contact, early in 1983, with what he describes as the "key life"—a priest/astronomer living in Central America over 1,000 years ago. The priest, says Currie, did not live up to his vow of celibacy and this led him, eventually, to stab a rival lover to death. Since examining this past life through the veil of a light hypnotic trance, Currie has experienced a gradual diminishing of the symptom as well as a growing awareness of reasons for certain depressive, authoritarian and ascetic personality characteristics. "The past-life images," says Currie, a former skeptic who came to believe in reincarnation after assessing the wealth of documented evidence, "carry a strong sense of emotional and intellectual conviction."

Currie feels that his interest in occult matters can be traced to this Central American existence where he failed to wield his power and influence responsibly. "I blew it," he confesses. "Now I am trying to advance knowledge of life after death in a more positive way." In four of the lives contacted so far in his continuing past-life inventory, Currie's wife, Margaret, has figured prominently, though not necessarily as marriage partner. Other relatives and friends have also made appearances.

The regressions have convinced Currie that his waning ailment is rooted in guilt repressed for centuries. He has also been assured of the long arm of karmic retribution. For after witnessing his knife murder in Central America all those years ago, he saw himself tortured, multilated and dispatched by a knife blade under similar circumstances while living as an Indian in the American south west before the Spanish conquest.

Déjà Vu

It happens seldom but it happens to almost all of us: an intestinal shock of recognition when encountering, ostensibly for the first time, a particular scene or individual. *Déjà vu* ("already seen") belies the presumed originality of all life experience and suggests the arousal of subconscious memories from other lives.

General George "Blood and Guts" Patton, America's irascible hero of World War II, was convinced he had lived before and backed up his claim with a wartime *déjà vu* experience at the French town of Langres. Patton was assuming his first command and a French liaison officer offered to show him around the town's fine Roman ruins. "You don't have to," Patton retorted. "I know this place. I know it well." Although the general had never been there before, he directed his driver around the ruins, pointing out the old amphitheatre, the drill ground, the forum and the temples of Mars and Apollo. Besides laying claim to having fought with Caesar's legions in a previous existence, Patton maintained he had reincarnated many times as a warrior. This conviction is forcibly expressed in a verse from his poem *Through a Glass Darkly*, written in 1944, the year before his death:

> So as through a glass and darkly
> The age-long strife I see
> Where I fought in many guises
> Many names—but always me!

Reflecting common experience, literary archives are replete with *déjà vu* episodes. For example, the poet Shelley, when walking with friends in a part of England he had never before visited, told a companion: "Over that hill there is a windmill." As they reached the top of the hill and were granted a view of the windmill he had described, Shelley fainted with emotion. The Scottish novelist Sir Walter Scott noted in his diary on February 17, 1828: "I cannot, I am sure, tell if it is worth marking down, that yesterday, at dinner time, I was strongly haunted by what I would call the sense of pre-existence, *viz.*, a confused idea that nothing that passed was said for the first time . . ." The first verse of Dante Gabriel Rossetti's poem *Sudden Light* strongly evokes the archetypal *déjà vu* experience:

> I have been here before,
> But when or how I cannot tell;
> I know the grass beyond the door,

The sweet keen smell,
The sighing sound, the lights around the shore.

As modern music superseded literature as the favorite form of sentimental expression, reincarnational references to *déjà vu* rode the airwaves. Crosby, Stills, Nash and Young built sweet, repetitive harmony around the idea in a 1970 album titled *Déjà Vu*. And, ten years later, Dionne Warwick enjoyed a smash hit with a song of the same name.

Past-Life Artistry

For past-life artist Isolde Bauer the incarnations are in the eyes. Staring into a person's eyes—be they alive or gazing from a photograph—she enters a trance with the aid of yoga breathing. Then she concentrates on the images the trance produces; images of her subject's previous existences. Gradually, the mind pictures, faces from the past, are translated to paper or canvas with her left hand. This, in itself, is extraordinary because Isolde is normally right-handed.

German-born Isolde, who now lives in Fresno, California, was originally a portrait painter who counted politicians and business people among her clientele. But in 1974 an out-of-body vision experienced while undergoing major surgery radically altered her way of working. "I felt as if a veil had been lifted from my eyes," she said. "Everything was bright and sharp. Colors were incredibly beautiful. When I looked at people, I could see the psychic energy of their auras. I began having flashes of past-life images flickering across the faces of those around me. When I told my friends what I was seeing, they kept asking me to describe their past lives. I decided that I would paint what I was seeing."

Isolde's paintings—which sell for $125 per individual or $195 for a couple—are composed of faces from other lives built around the present likeness. A past-life reading accompanies each portrait which is executed in monochromatic black or brown charcoal, oils, pastels, acrylics—whatever medium the subject prefers. Usually, Isolde works from photographs in the quiet surroundings of her home. "The eyes are the key," she insists. "When I get the eyes done the way I want them, the past-life images begin to reveal themselves. The modern day face changes for a split-second. In many ways it is an automatic process—I merely get things started and then the painting constructs itself." Isolde maintains that most of her subjects—who include such metaphysical heavyweights as Dick Sutphen, Hans Holzer and Peter Hurkos—are gripped with a sense of familiarity on seeing their past-life grouping.

The ability to see faces in split-second transformation is not confined to Isolde Bauer and her past-life artistry. Clinical psychologist Ronald Wong Jue of Fullerton, California, tends to see people in past-life images while working to relieve psychosomatic illness. "I focus on the energy of my clients and the images come," says Dr. Jue. "It's an inner movie in my mind. Sometimes, when my clients share the image, they go into a regression. It's an intuitive approach."

Sixty-seven-year-old British hypnotherapist Jo Kirby will never forget the awakening of her clairvoyant powers one day in June, 1980. She was traveling on the London subway and her head was reeling from the sudden transformation in the people seated nearby. A pretty girl in a short dress became a tramp with a chin of grey stubble. A plump, middle-aged housewife was changed into a much younger woman in a nun's habit. And a young man, dressed casually in T-shirt and jeans, appeared as a last-century naval officer dressed in a uniform with brass buttons. "It was like a fancy dress party," Jo Kirby recalls. "And it ended up driving me mad. After a lot of meditation I eventually found a way of shutting off the images."

The Population Conundrum

Critics of rebirth like nothing better than to point at the fast-rising world population and exclaim: "If reincarnation is a fact, where do all these 'new' people come from?" Certainly, the global population doubled from A.D. 25 to 1500, doubled again by 1800, and has more than quadrupled since then. But the skeptics fail to take into account the length of the between-life or *bardo* state which, the evidence from hypnosis suggests, has been steadily diminishing as world change has accelerated. This alone could create the rise in population. It might well be that when there was little change from generation to generation entities chose longer breaks between incarnations, whereas today's rapid advances act as a magnet for souls ever hungry for new experiences.

Dr. Edith Fiore's hypnotherapy casebook tells her that anyone under forty years of age has probably lived before during this century, while many people are experiencing their third or fourth life since 1900. Dr. Helen Wambach, whose subjects have reported increasingly shorter periods out of incarnation as they made pointed references to impending global destruction, says of the current burgeoning population: "In my own mind, I liken it to the cast of a musical gathering onstage for the finale." One of Dr. Wambach's studies, involving 1,100 people who were invited to locate at random three incarnations from ten time periods scattered across 4,000 years, reproduced the estimated upward population curve of the Earth. The hypnotized subjects apparently demonstrated that increasingly faster reincarnations have boosted population figures over the last few centuries. Leading Theosophist Dr. Annie Besant noted in 1893 that the answer to the vexing population growth question lies in the number of unbodily egos always being "enormously greater" than those incarnate. She wrote:

> The globe is as a small hall in a large town, drawing the audiences that enter it from the total population. It may be at one time half empty, at another crowded, without any change in the total population of the town.

Not to be left out of the debate are the supposed additions to and subtractions from the human race—entities graduating to human bodies from the animal kingdom and the rebirth of highly evolved humans on a higher plane. Joe Keeton is quick to point out that as the human population rises, the animal population goes down. "Where have all those pieces of life force gone?" he asks. "Is that where we get such human beings as concentration camp guards?"

Dr. Ian Stevenson notes that plausible estimates of the total number of people who have lived on earth range from 69 billion to 96 billion. This would leave each member of the human race—currently estimated at 4.8 billion people—with approximately 15 to 20 past lives.

15

Bringing It All Back Home

A person whose life's vision is limited to this one fleeting incarnation is like the plow horse which views its life work as a single furrow, never able to appreciate how one furrow blends with the many others.

BRYAN JAMEISON

It is not enough to know about reincarnation; we must live it.

GUENTHER WACHSMUTH

The narrow prospect is detonated, the walls come tumbling down and, suddenly, everything makes sense. It's like being relieved of the misapprehension that one day is not an entire lifetime after all; that human existence is much vaster, much grander and invested with far greater meaning than one could possibly have imagined.

In extending one life to many lives, reincarnation grants significance to each existence, just as a lifetime of personal development counts on each day's vital contribution. Hope

159

accompanies this broader vision. Not naive, idealistic hope, but hope founded on a blending of faith and reason. Reincarnation tells us that even the most tragic, sordid deaths are just more births in the making, and that nothing can ever happen on the myriad journeys of unfoldment except opportunities to learn and grow. So it is that lives on Earth, shaped by karmic propensities, become charged with meaning. Each thought, word and deed is rich with purpose as it bears the cause of effect to come. And this brings home the truth that we are thoroughly responsible and accountable for who we are and what we do; that we can't blame circumstance, or external forces of any kind, for our lot in life. We make our beds, as the saying goes, and we must lie in them.

Although the lives of well-heeled criminals and poverty-stricken saints suggest a dearth of justice in the world, justice becomes apparent in the wider context granted by a succession of existences. Only through many lives can joy and misery and the glaring inequalities of life be justified. Words such as "coincidence," "accident" and "unfairness" lose their currency as the individual accepts that he or she has generated every action and reaction along the way. Reincarnation means that each of us is partaking in an ultimately joyous progression of self-realization spanning an incalculable number of embodiments. A sense of incompletion instils a craving for experience which keeps bringing us back until our potential is fulfilled in perfection. Destinies shaped individually merge and interact with the collective destinies of families, groups of like-minded people, nations and the world at large. This is how we grow.

As Natural as Breathing

There's nothing extraordinary about reincarnation. It's as natural as breathing and just as compatible with the unceasing ebb and flow of the universe. Unfortunately, our protracted alienation from primordial rhythms and our brainwashing by materialism's false assumptions cause rebirth to be seen by many as a quaint indulgence, a corollary of wishful thinking held by the eccentric and the simple-minded.

Yet consider the transformation of earthly existence were

reincarnation accepted into the soulstream of the global population as a guide by which to live. Acutely aware of reaping harvests of past deeds while simultaneously sowing the seeds of future lives, most people would behave very differently. Life on the planet would be overhauled—and hugely for the better. Wars, crime, racism, nationalism and sexual chauvinism would be radically diminished. For who can harm, or harbor prejudice against the kind of person one has been or will be, especially if retribution can follow in another life? The nagging fear of death would be eliminated and replaced with acceptance of the opportunity for transformation. Doctors who strive to prolong life with the aid of every available artificial means would see themselves as sad clowns flaunting their ignorance of cosmic renewal. Few would be so rash as to attempt either suicide or abortion, and genetic engineering would be recognized by all as meddlesome and dangerous. Care would be taken not to encourage the extinction of animal and plant species lest rungs be removed from the evolutionary ladder. And those who consign their corpses to graves of ice in hope of subsequent technological resuscitation would acknowledge they are wasting their money in trying to preserve the old body when they stand to inherit a new one free of charge!

Acceptance of reincarnation demands a complete overturning of prevailing attitudes inculcated by a civilization that has long overidentified with the body. This overidentification is locked into our very language. We say, for example, "I am hungry" when we mean to say, as some Indians *do* say, "My body is hungry." Annie Besant comments in *Reincarnation*:

> If we were in the habit of identifying ourselves in thought, not with the habitation we live in but with the Human Self that dwells therein, life would become a greater and serener thing. We should brush off troubles as we brush the dust from our garments, and we should realize that the measure of all things happening to us is not the pain or pleasure they bring to our bodies, but the progress or retardation they bring to the Man within us; and since all things are matters of experience and lessons may be learned from each, we should take the sting out of griefs by

searching in each for the wisdom enwrapped in it as the petals are folded within the bud.

Similarly, the urgency and anxiety springing from the race against time evaporate once we realize we have all the time and all the lives we need. Eternity is our heritage and reincarnation, requiring worldly time for its expression, gives time freely. To steep oneself in infinity brings nothing but exhilaration. Nobody is pretending that psychic surrender to adverse conditions and the seeming ravages of time is easy to accomplish as we cope with the daily vicissitudes of the material world. But a certain serenity should ensue if Goethe's "continual law of Die and Be Again" can be absorbed into our being. For the value and the power of reincarnation cannot be discovered by examining the theory like a fossil under glass or by toying intellectually with its precepts. It must be lived. And this entails a rebirth of the way we think and feel; the metamorphosis that follows from truly believing we are immortal beings forging our souls through a multitude of lifetimes on the global anvil.

For all the evidence of past lives and future lives and for all the speculation about worlds being reborn across aeons of time, reincarnation addresses itself most pointedly to the present moment. While other lives and other ages take care of themselves, the present is all we have and always the only available life is this one. Nothing ever matters but the *now* with its marvellous incorporation of all reincarnational history. For even as we are today what we established yesterday, we will surely be tomorrow what we establish today. Therein lies the challenge of reincarnation—a challenge that prompted this advice from the great German philosopher Friedrich Nietzsche:

Live so that thou mayest desire to live again—that is thy duty—for in any case thou wilt live again!

Bibliography

Books

Aquarian Gospel of Jesus the Christ, The, (Transcribed from the Akashic Records), Marina Del Rey, Cal.: DeVorss & Co., 1981.

Arroyo, Stephen, *Astrology, Karma and Transformation*. Davis, California: CRCS Publications, 1978.

Aurobindo, Sri, *The Problem of Rebirth*. Pondicherry, India. Sri Aurobindo Ashram Trust, 1973.

Bailey, Alice A., *Esoteric Astrology*. New York: Lucis Publishing Company, 1979.

———, *The Light of the Soul*. New York: Lucis Publishing Company.

Banerjee, H. N., *Americans Who Have Been Reincarnated*. New York: Macmillan, 1980.

Banerjee, H. N. and Oursler, Will, *Lives Unlimited*. New York: Doubleday, 1974.

Barlow, Fred, *Mental Prodigies*. London: Hutchinson's, 1952.

Bennett, Colin, *Practical Time Travel*, London: Rider, 1937.

Bernstein, Morey, *The Search For Bridey Murphy*. New York: Pocket Books, 1978.

Besant, Annie, *Reincarnation*. Madras, India: The Theosophical Publishing House, 1975.

Besterman, Theodore, *Collected Papers on the Paranormal*. New York: Garrett, 1968.

Blavatsky, H. P., *The Secret Doctrine*, Los Angeles: The Theosophy Company.

Brandon, S. G. F., *Religion in Ancient History*. New York: Charles Scribner's & Sons, 1969.

Brennan, J. H., *Reincarnation: Five Keys to Past Lives*. Wellingborough, Northants: The Aquarian Press, 1981.

Brunhübner, Fritz (translated by Julie Baum), *Pluto*. Washington: American Federation of Astrologers, 1949.

Campbell, Joseph, *The Masks of God: Oriental Mythology*. New York: Viking Press, 1962.

———, *The Masks of God: Primitive Mythology*. New York: Viking Press, 1959.

Cannon, Dr. Alexander, *The Power Within*. London: Rider and Company, 1950.

———, *Powers That Be*. London: Francis Mott Company, 1934.

Capra, Fritjof, *The Tao of Physics*. New York: Bantam Books, 1980.

Carr, Donald E., *The Eternal Return*. New York: Doubleday, 1968.

Catholic Encyclopaedia, The. New York: Robert Appleton Company, 1911.

Cavendish, Richard, ed., *Man, Myth and Magic*. (Vols 12, 17). London: Marshall Cavendish Corporation, 1970.

Cerminara, Gina, *Many Mansions*. New York: William Sloane, 1956.

Chuang Tzu, The Musings of a Chinese Mystic. London: John Murray, 1955.

Christie-Murray, David, *Reincarnation: Ancient Beliefs and Modern Evidence*. Newton Abbot, Devon: David and Charles, 1981.

Cohen, Daniel, *The Mysteries of Reincarnation*. New York: Dodd Mead, 1975.

Crowley, Aleister, *Magick*. New York: Weiser, 1979.

Dethlefsen, Thorwald, *Voices from Other Lives*. New York: M. Evans and Co., 1977.

Easton, Stewart C., *Man and World in the Light of Anthroposophy*. New York: The Anthroposophic Press, 1975.

Eberhard, Wolfram, *Chinese Festivals*. New York: H. Schuman, 1952.

Eliade, Mircea, *Rites and Symbols of Initiation*. New York: Harper Torchbooks, 1958.

Evans-Wentz, W. Y., *The Fairy Faith in Celtic Countries*, London: Oxford University Press, 1911.,

———, ed., *The Tibetan Book of the Dead*, London: Oxford University Press, 1960.

———, ed., *Tibet's Great Yogi Milarepa*. London: Oxford University Press, 1974.

Ferguson, John, *An Illustrated Encyclopaedia of Mysticism*. London: Thames and Hudson, 1976.

Fiore, Dr. Edith, *You Have Been Here Before*. New York: Coward, McCann and Geoghegan, 1978.

Ford, Arthur (as told to Jerome Ellison), *The Life Beyond Death*. New York: Berkley Medallion Books, 1972.

Frazer, Sir James George, *The Belief in Immortality*. (Vol. 2), London: Dawsons of Pall Mall, 1968.

———, *Folk-Lore in the Old Testament*. London: Macmillan, 1918.

———, *The Golden Bough*, London: Macmillan, 1963.

Fremantle, Francesca and Trungpa, Chogyam, *The Tibetan Book of the Dead*. Boulder, Colorado: Shambala Publications, 1975.

Furst, Peter J., *Stones, Bones and Skin: Ritual and Shamanic Art*. Toronto, Ont.: The Society for Art Publications, 1977.

Gallup, Dr. George, Jr., *Adventures in Immortality*. New York: McGraw-Hill, 1982.

Gaskell, G.A., *Dictionary of All Scriptures and Myths*. New York: Julian Press, 1977.

Glaskin, G.M., *A Door to Eternity*. London: Wildwood House, 1979.

———, *Windows of the Mind*. New York: Delacorte Press, 1974.

Goldberg, Dr. Bruce, *Past Lives, Future Lives*, North Hollywood, Cal.: Newcastle Publishing, 1982.

Grant, Joan, *Far Memory*. New York: Harper and Row, 1956.

Gray, Louis Herbert, ed., *The Mythology of All Races*. Boston: Marshall Jones, 1918.

Gribbin, John, *White Holes*. New York: Delacorte Press, 1977.

Gris, Henry and Dick, William, *The New Soviet Psychic Discoveries*. Englewood Cliffs, N.J.: Prentice Hall, 1978.

Groff, Stanislav, *Varieties of Transpersonal Experiences: Observations from LSD Psychotheraphy*. Chicago: Nelson-Hall, 1975.

Grof, Stanislav and Grof, Christina, *Beyond Death*. New York: Thames and Hudson, 1980.

Guirdham, Arthur, *The Psyche in Medicine*. Jersey: Neville Spearman, 1978.

Gunaratna, V. F., *Rebirth Explained*. Kandy, Sri Lanka: Buddhist Publication Society, 1971.

Hall, Manly P., *Reincarnation, The Cycle of Necessity*. Los Angeles: The Philosophical Research Society, 1978.

Harrer, Heinrich, *Seven Years in Tibet*. London: Pan Books, 1956.

Hastings, James, ed., *Encyclopaedia of Religion and Ethics*. Edinburgh: T. and T. Clark, 1934.

Head, Joseph and Cranston, S.L., eds., *Reincarnation: The Phoenix Fire Mystery*. New York: Crown Publishers, 1977.

Hickey, Isabel M., *Pluto or Minerva: The Choice Is Yours*. Watertown, Mass.: Fellowship House Bookshop, 1977.

Holzer, Hans, *Patterns of Destiny*. Los Angeles: Nash Publishing, 1974.

Howe, Quincy, Jr., *Reincarnation for the Christian*. Philadelphia: The Westminster Press, 1974.

Humphreys, Christmas, *Karma and Rebirth*. London: John Murray, 1943.

Jameison, Bryan, *Explore Your Past Lives*. Van Nuys, Cal.: Astro-Analytics Publications, 1976.

Jast, L. Stanley, *What It All Means*. London: T. Werner Laurie, 1941.

Johnston, Charles, *The Memory of Past Births*. New York: Metaphysical Publishing, 1899.

Judge, William Q., *The Ocean of Theosophy*. Los Angeles: Theosophy Company, [n.d.].

Kelsey, Denys and Grant, Joan, *Many Lifetimes*. New York: Doubleday, 1967.

Langley, Noel, *Edgar Cayce on Reincarnation*. London: Howard Baker, 1969.

Laws of Manu, The. Delhi, India: Motilal Banarsidass, 1967.

Leek, Sybil, *Reincarnation: The Second Chance*. New York: Stein and Day, 1974.

Lenz, Frederic, *Lifetimes*. New York: The Bobbs-Merrill Company, 1979.

Lowell, Laurel, *Pluto*. St. Paul, Minn.: Llewellyn Publications, 1973.

McDermott, Robert A., ed., *The Essential Aurobindo*. New York: Schocken Books, 1973.

Moody, Dr. Raymond A., Jr., *Life After Life*. New York: Bantam Books, 1981.

Moore, Marcia and Douglas, Mark, *Reincarnation: Key to Immortality*. York Cliffs, Maine: Arcane Publications, 1968.

Moore, Marcia and Alltounian, Howard Sunny, *Journeys into the Bright World*. Rockport, Mass.: Para Research, 1978.

Morris, Ivan, *The Nobility of Failure*. New York: Holt, Rinehart and Winston, 1975.

Moss, Peter with Keeton, Joe, *Encounters with the Past*. New York: Penguin, 1981.

Müller, Ernst, *History of Jewish Mysticism*, Oxford: Phaidon Press, 1946.

Müller, Max, ed., *The Scared Books of the East*, London: Oxford University Press, 1880–1890.

Netherton, Morris and Schiffrin, Nancy, *Past Lives Therapy*. New York: William Morrow, 1978.

Ouspensky, P. D., *A New Model of the Universe*. New York: Vintage Books, 1971.

Parameswara, P., *Soul, Karma and Re-birth*. Bangalore: P. Parameswara, 1973.

Parrinder, Geoffrey, *The Indestructible Soul*. New York: Harper and Row, 1973.

Patanjali, Bhagwan Shree, *Aphorisms of Yoga*. London: Faber and Faber, 1973.

Perry, W.J., *The Origin of Magic and Religion*. Port Washington, N.Y.: Kennikat Press, 1923.

Prabhupada, His Divine Grace A.C. Bhaktivedanta Swami, *Bhagavad-Gita As It Is*. New York: The Bhaktivedanta Book Trust, 1976.

Pryse, James M., *Reincarnation in the New Testament*. New York: Elliot B. Page, 1900.

Ram Dass, *Grist For the Mill*. Santa Cruz: Unity Press, 1977.

———, *The Only Dance There Is*. New York: Anchor Press, 1974.

Reyna, Dr. Ruth, *Reincarnation and Science*. New Delhi: Sterling Publishers, 1973.

Ring, Kenneth, *Life At Death*. New York: Coward, McCann and Geoghegan, 1980.

Roberts, Jane, *The Nature of Personal Reality*. Englewood Cliffs, N.J.: Prentice-Hall, 1974.

———, *The Seth Material*, New York: Bantam Books, 1981.

Rudhyar, Dane, *An Astrological Triptych*. New York: Asi Publishers, 1968.

Ruperti, Alexander, *Cycles of Becoming*. Davis, Cal.: CRCS Publications, 1978.

Russell, Jeffrey B., *A History of Witchcraft*. New York: Thames and Hudson, 1980.

Schecter, Jerrold, *The New Face of Buddha*. New York: Coward-McCann, 1967.

Seward, Jack, *Hara-Kiri: Japanese Ritual Suicide*. Tokyo: Charles E. Tuttle Co., 1968.

Shepard, Leslie, ed., *Encyclopaedia of Occultism and Parapsychology*. Detroit: Gale Research Co.

Sivananda, Swami, *What Becomes of the Soul after Death*. Himalayas, India: Divine Life Society, 1972.

Smart, Ninian, *The Long Search*. Boston: Little, Brown and Co., 1980.

Spencer, Sir Baldwin, *Native Tribes of the Northern Territory of Australia*. London, 1914.

Steiner, Rudolf, *An Outline of Occult Science*. Spring Valley, N.Y.: Antroposophic Press.

Stevenson, Dr. Ian. *Cases of the Reincarnation Type* (Vols. 1–3). Charlottesville: University Press of Virginia.

———, *Twenty Cases Suggestive of Reincarnation*. Charlottesville: University Press of Virginia, 1974.

Stokes, Henry Scott, *The Life and Death of Yukio Mishima*.
Tokyo: Charles E. Tuttle Co., 1975.

Sutphen, Dick, *Past Lives, Future Loves*. New York: Pocket
Books, 1978.

Tatz, Mark and Kent, Jody, *Rebirth: The Tibetan Game of
Liberation*. New York: Anchor Press, 1977.

Toyne, Clarice, *Heirs To Eternity*. London: Neville Spearman, 1976.

Verny, Dr. Thomas, with Kelly, John, *The Secret Life of the
Unborn Child*. Don Mills, Ont.: Collins Publishers, 1981.

Wachsmuth, Guenther, *Reincarnation as a Phenomenon of
Metamorphosis*. New York: Anthroposophic Press, 1937.

Walker, Benjamin, *Hindu World*. London: George Allen and
Unwin, 1968.

———, *Masks of the Soul*. Wellingborough, Northants: The
Aquarian Press, 1981.

Walker, E. D., *Reincarnation: A Study of Forgotten Truth*.
New York: Theosophical Publishing Co., 1904.

Wambach, Helen, *Life Before Life*. New York: Bantam Books,
1979.

———, *Reliving Past Lives: The Evidence Under Hypnosis*.
New York: Harper and Row, 1978.

Wangdu, Sonam, *The Discovery of the XIVth. Dalai Lama*.
Bangkok: Klett Thai Publications, 1975.

Weatherhead, Leslie D., *The Christian Agnostic*. London:
Hodder and Stoughton, 1965.

Weisman, Alan, *We, Immortals*. New York: Pocket Books,
1979.

Wilber, Ken, *The Spectrum of Consciousness*. Wheaton, Ill.:
The Theosophical Publishing House, 1977.

Wilson, Colin, *The Occult*. New York: Random House, 1971.

Wilson, Ian, *Mind Out of Time?* London: Victor Gollancz
Ltd., 1981.

Zukav, Gary, *The Dancing Wu Li Masters: An Overview of
the New Physics*. New York: Bantam Books, 1980.

Periodicals and Pamphlets

Banerjee, H. N., "Murderer and Victim Meet," _Fate_, February, 1980.

Bannister, Paul, "Dead Man Lives Again in This Girl's Body," _National Enquirer_, October 6, 1981.

Bowen, Francis, "Christian Metempsychosis," _Princeton Review_, May, 1881.

Crehan, Father J. H., _Reincarnation_. Catholic Truth Society, London.

Crenshaw, James, "Xenoglossy—Proof of Reincarnation?" _Fate_, July, 1981.

Denton, Jon, "The Mysterious Memories of Jeremy," _The Sunday Oklahoman_, April 27, 1980.

Downer, Craig C., "Do Animals Reincarnate?" _Reincarnation Report_, October, 1982.

Duffy, David, "Tragedy of the Rabbit Fantasy Boy," _Sunday Mirror_, April 4, 1976.

Edvardsen, Annu, "Lilla Romy Moter Sin Mor Fran Sitt Tidigare Liv," _Allers_, Helsingborg, Sweden, April 19, 1981.

Gribbin, John, "Does the Universe Oscillate?" _Astronomy_, August, 1977.

Herron, Vanessa, "Of Kingfisher, Okla, and the Nine Lives of Ernie Shafenberg," _The Wall Street Journal_, August 31, 1981.

Journal of Nervous and Mental Disease, "Commentary on Dr. Ian Stevenson's 'The Evidence of Man's Survival After Death,'" Vol. 165, No. 3, September, 1977.

Koenig, William J., "Something To Think About," _The Compensator_, November, 1966.

Lewis, Emanuel, "Inhibition of Mourning by Pregnancy: Psycopathology and Management," _British Medical Journal_, July 7, 1979.

Meltzoff, Andrew N., and M. Keith Moore, "Imitation of Facial and Manual Gestures by Human Neonates," *Science*, October 7, 1977.

Plimpton, George, "Interview with Sylvester Stallone," *People Weekly*, June 21, 1982.

Psychic News, "Bird of Passage Is Reincarnated Husband, Says Wife," August 22, 1970.

———, "Dowding Stands By Reincarnation," November 3, 1945.

The Rosicrucian Digest, "The Experience of Reincarnation," Parts 1, 2 and 3, October, November and December, 1979.

Stevenson, Dr. Ian, "The Explanatory Value of the Idea of Reincarnation," *Journal of Nervous and Mental Disease*, Vol. 164, 1977.

———, "Some Questions Related to Cases of the Reincarnation Type," *Journal of the American Society for Psychical Research*, Vol. 68, 1974.

———, "The Southeast Asian Interpretation of Gender Dysphoria: An Illustrative Case Report," *Journal of Nervous and Mental Disease*, Vol. 165, 1977.

Sunday People, The, " 'Second Life' of a Gipsy," May 28, 1978.

Theosophy Company, The, *Reincarnation and Karma*, Los Angeles, 1923.

Time Magazine, "Going Gentle Into That Good Night," March 21, 1983.

Times, The, "The Controversial and the Problematical," December 20, 1980.

Touby, Frank, "Born Again," *Today Magazine*, October 4, 1980.

Viereck, George Sylvester, "Interview with Henry Ford," *San Francisco Examiner*, August 27, 1928.

Wambach, Helen, "Pleasures and Perils of Reincarnation Research," *Fate*, April, 1981.

Whitton, Joel L., "Hypnotic Time Regression and Reincarnation Memories," *New Horizons*, June, 1976.

————, "Karma in Reincarnation," *The Rosicrucian Digest*, October, 1978.

————, "Xenoglossia: A Subject with Two Possible Instances," *New Horizons*, September, 1978.

Tapes

Buckley, Dr. Paul, "Interview with Dr. Ian Stevenson," Toronto, Ont.: Canadian Broadcasting Corporation, 1976.

"The Reincarnation Experiment," Sydney, Australia: Channel 7 and *The Sun*, March 22 and 23, 1983.

Kaplan, Dr. Pascal, "Reincarnation: Rediscovering a Lost Teaching." Lecture given at John F. Kennedy University, Orinda, California, 1980.

Index

A

Aborigines, 24, 60–61, 84
abortion, 40, 161
Adams, Richard, 102
ahimsa, 103
Akashic Records, The,
   137–138, 149
Alexander, Hartley, B., 99
Alexander the Great, 53
Alger, William, 74
Alltounian, Dr. Howard, 81
Anderson, Jeremy, 15–16
animals, rebirth as, 95–108,
   139
Anthroposophy, 23–24, 85
Arroyo, Stephen, 123
Arthur, King, 53
Association for Past Life
   Research and Ther-
   apy, 41, 50
astrology and rebirth,
   118–27
astro-physics, 22–23
Atlantis, 54, 123, 150
Audrey Rose, 26

Aurobindo, Sri, 95, 108
Aztecs, The, 52, 112, 149

B

babies, imitating, 29, 30
babies, stillborn, 62
Bach, Richard, 101
Bailey, Alice A., 20, 138
Baker, Margaret, 47–48
Balzac, Honoré De, 25
Banerjee, Hemendra, 6, 8,
   11–12, 17–18
Barddas, 57, 96
Bardo Thödol, 76–77, 78–79,
   80–81, 82, 87–88
Barker, William, J., 47
Bellamy, Edward, 147
Bennett, Colin, 129, 134,
   136
Bernstein, Morey, 3, 46
Besant, Dr. Annie, 158, 163
between life state, the,
   76–88, 157–58
Bhagavad-Gita, 23, 53,
   109, 111

Bible, The, 2, 23, 27, 58, 66, 71–73
birthmarks, 12–13
Björkhem, John, 43
Blake, Maurice, 47
Blavatsky, Madame H. P., 76, 85
Brahmins, 53, 98
Brennan, J. H., 129, 137
Brown, Bonnie, 44–45
Bruno, Giordano, 23
Brunhübner, Fritz, 117, 123
Brunton, Paul, 131
Buddha, Gautama, 55–56, 130
Buddhaghosha, 130–131

C

cabins, initiatory, 63
Caesar, Julius, 111
Campbell, Joseph, 82
cannibalism, 61–62, 104
Cannon, Dr. Alexander, 43
Capablanca, Jose, 28
Capra, Fritjof, 21
Cardiac, Jean Louis, 27
Cayce, Edgar, 3, 28, 121, 137, 148–50
Celts, The, 57, 110–11
Cerminara, Gina, 150, 164
Chand, Bishen, 9–10
Chang and Eng, 29
Chenrizeg, 144, 146
Chogyam Trungpa, *Rinpoche*, 76
Christianity, 2, 58, 65–75, 119
Christos Experience, The, 138–40
Cicero, 26–83
clairvoyance, 51, 91, 123, 157

Columbus, Christopher, 119
Comet, Halley's, 119
Constantine, Emperor, 67
Constantinople, Second Council of, 69–70
Crees, Romy, 5–8
Crehan, Father Joseph, 75
Crowley, Aleister, 128, 130, 132–34, 143
cryptomnesia, 12
Currie, Ian, 153–54

D

da Gama, Vasco, 119
Dalai Lama, The, 144–46
De Felitta, Raymond, 4, 25
dé jà vu, 17, 154–56
De La Vega, Garcilasso, 104
de Marco, Giannella, 28
Denning, Hazel, 50
de Rochas, Col. Albert, 42
Descartes, Rene, 26
Dethlefsen, Thorwald, 87, 152
devachan, 85
Dictionary of All Scriptures and Myths, 65
dreams, 17, 36, 91, 136
Druids, The, 57, 110–11

E

Edelstein, Dr. Gerald, 37
Egyptian Book of the Dead, The, 99
Einstein, Albert, 21
Eisler, Robert, 118
Eleusinian Mysteries, 56
Eliade, Mircea, 63
Elijah, 72
Emerson, Ralph Waldo, 89
epilepsy, 82, 86

Eskimos, 60, 105
Essenes, The, 110–11
Evans-Wentz, W. Y., 52–53
evolution, 4, 96, 106–8, 123
exercises, past-life, 130–42

F

fanany, 104
fantasy, 6, 37
Fiore, Dr. Edith, 37, 40–42, 87, 152, 158
fraud, 11
Frazer, Sir James George, 59
Freud, Sigmund, 43
future lives, 91–94

G

Galileo, 19
Gallup Poll, 4
Gandhi, Mohandas K., 34
Gauss, Carl Friedrich, 28
genetic engineering, 161
George, William, 12–13
Glaskin, Gerry, 138–39
Gnostics, The, 58, 65–66, 69
Godaigo, Emperor, 112
Goldberg, Dr. Bruce, 93
Grant, Joan, 90
Greene, Liz, 122
Grey, Sir George, 61
Gribbin, John, 22
Grof, Dr. Stanislav, 32, 81, 97–98
group reincarnation, 33, 44
Guirdham, Dr. Arthur, 35, 43–44

H

Haeckel's Law, 105–7
Hainlen, John, 49
Hall, Manly P., 96, 109

hara-kiri, 112–14
Harrer, Heinrich, 102
Hawken, Paul, 97
Heinecken, Christian Friedrich, 27
Henderson, Cynthia, 48
Herder, J.G., 5
heredity, 29, 31–32
Herodotus, 57
Hickey, Isabel M., 121
Hinduism, 2, 3, 53–56, 99, 131
Holzer, Hans, 70
Huddar, Uttara, 151–52
Hugo, Victor, 1
Humber, John, 122
Huxley, Thomas Henry, 31–32
hypnosis, 35–50, 88, 92, 152–54

I

I Ching, The, 125
Incas, The, 112, 149
Indians, North American, 52, 59, 62, 103–4, 105, 110, 111
Isao Matsuo, 113
Ivanova, Varvara, 45

J

Jains, The, 102–3
Jalalu' L-Din Rumi, 95
Jameison, Bryan, 87, 140–41, 159
James, William, 88
Janus, Beverly, 44
Jayaratne, Sujuth Lakmal, 31
Jayasena, Gamini, 31

Jesus Christ, 58, 65–67, 72–74, 83, 118, 149, 150
Johnston, Charles, 142
John the Baptist, 72
Josephus, Flavius, 110
Judiasm, 57–58
Judge, William Q., 71
Jue, Dr. Ronald Wong, 157
Jung, Carl, 51

K

Kabala, The, 58, 99
kama loka, 85
kamikaze pilots, 113–14
Kaplan, Dr. Pascal, 75
karma, 2, 4, 29, 41, 54, 73, 78, 84–85, 120, 122, 125, 149, 154
Keenan, Caroline, 125–27
Keeton, Joe, 47, 50, 97, 158
Ketamine, 81
Kirby, Jo, 157
Kleppe-Moran, Shirley, 45
Knight, William, 25
Knights Templars, 71
Koenig, William, 118–19
Koran, The, 57
Krishna, 53, 111
Kübler-Ross, Dr. Elizabeth, 33, 79

L

Lammers, Arthurs, 149
Leek, Sybil, 106
Lenz, Frederic, 80
Lethe, River, 83
Lief, Dr. Harold, 19
Life extension, 161
Lorenz, Paulo, 115
Lowell, Laurel, 122

Lowell, Percival, 122
LSD, 32, 80–81, 97–98

M

Maclean, Dorothy, 96–97
Mantilla, Miguel, 27
Manu, Laws of, 98–99
Martin, The Rev. John, 63
Masashige, Kusunoki, 112–13
Ma Tin Aung Myo, 13–15
Mayo, Marie, 42
McLuhan, Marshall, 49
memory, extracerebral, 6
memory, past-life, 35–50, 152–154
memory, past-life (among children), 5–18
Meng P'o, 83
Mesmer, Franz Anton, 42
Milinda's Questions, 56
Mill, John Stuart, 28
minerals and rebirth, 95–108
Mirandola, Pico della, 64
Mishima, Yukio, 114
Mitra, Dolan, 13–14
moksha, 54
Moody, Dr. Raymond, 79, 87
moon, the, 24
Moore, Marcia, 81
Morrison, Al, 126
Mozart, Wolfgang Amadeus, 27
Murphy, Bridey, 3, 45–47, 87
Myers, Frederic, 108
Myers, Joe, 147–48

N

Neanderthal society, 52
Nebuchadnezzar, King, 99

Netherton, Dr. Morris, 35, 38–40, 45, 87, 97, 152

Newman, H.H., 29

New physics, xiii, 21, 24

Newton, Sir Isaac, 2, 50

Nietzsche, Friedrich, 162

O

Oliviero, Sinha, 148

Origen, 66–67, 69

Orphic Mysteries, 57

Osiris, 53, 57

Ouspensky, P. D., 32

out-of-body experiences, 76, 78–83, 87

Ovid, 100

oxytocin, 84

P

palingenesis, 20

Pasricha, Dr. Satwant, 151–52

Patanjali, 132

Patton, General George, 155

Paul, Saint, 23, 72

Percival, Harold W., 148

Persephone, 56, 121

phobias, 36, 37

Pickering, Helen, 48

Pinart, Alphonse, 111

Pistis Sophia, 56, 73, 83

plants and rebirth, 95–108

Plato, 26, 57, 83, 99

Plotinus, 83, 100

Pluto, xii, 117–27

Pluto/Scorpio Age, xii, 118–27

population, distribution of, 37, 157–58

prodigies, 25–29

punabbhava, 55

Pythagoras, 57, 99–100

Q

Quetzalcoatl, 52

Quiché Maya, 53

R

rainbow serpent, 60

Ralston, Josephine, 101–2

Rama, 53

Ram Dass, 33–34, 89

Ramster, Peter, 48

Ramu, 17

Reincarnation Experiments, The, 48

Reincarnation Report, 75, 91

Renaissance, 3, 119

relativity, theories of, 21

Richet, Dr. Charles, 151

Rig-Veda, The, 82

Ring, Dr. Kenneth, 79

Roberts, Jane, 86

Rosicrucians, The, 71, 96, 136

Rossetti, Dante Gabriel, 155

Ross, Nancy, 55

Rudhyar, Dane, 124

Rufinus, 71

Ruperti, Alexander, 117, 123–24

S

samsara, 21, 77

scalping, 61–62

schizophrenia, 81, 88

Schopenhauer, Arthur, 7

Schultze-Jena, Leonhard, 52

Search, 116

Seth, 86, 90

Shakespeare, William, 101

shamanism, 52, 82
Shea, Steven, 102
Shelley, 155
Shiva, 21
Sivananda, Sri Swami, 106
Socrates, 20, 26
Solow, Victor, 80
soma, 82
Song of Olaf Ostesen, 83
spirit possession, 4, 12, 36–37
Staden, Hans, 104
Steiner, Rudolf, 4, 23, 132
Stevenson, Dr. Ian, 5, 9, 12–13, 16–19, 31, 115, 151–52, 158
subatomic particles, 21
suicide, 114–16, 161
Sutphen, Dick, 47, 93–94, 157
symbols of rebirth, 135–36

T
Tacitus, 110
Tao, 21
Tatenokai, 114
Theodosius, Emperor, 68
Theosophy, 3, 71, 85
Thessalonica, The Edict of, 68
therapy, past-life, 35–50, 152–54
Thoreau, Henry David, xiii
Tiberius, Emperor, 119
Tibetan Book of the Dead, The, 76–78, 79, 80, 82, 88, 99
Tibetans, 61, 76–77, 135, 144–46
Tolstoy, Leo, 115
Toyne, Clarice, 129, 147–48

transmigration, 57, 59, 99
tribal memory, 59–64
troubadours, 71
Trungpa, Chogyam, 88

U
Upanishad, Katha, 54
Upanishad, Svetasvatara, 54

V
Vaughan, Alan, 91
vegetarianism, 103
Verny, Dr. Thomas, 30–31, 39
Vigilius, Pope, 69
Virgil, 83
Vogel, Marcel, 96
Voltaire, 3

W
Wachsmuth, Guenther, 115–16, 159
Walker, E. D., 51, 58
Wambach, Dr. Helen, 15, 33, 37, 45, 49, 87, 92, 97, 158
warriors and rebirth, 109–14
Weatherhead, Dr. Leslie, 74
wheel of life, 2, 54, 57, 64, 77, 160
Whitton, Dr. Joel, 152–53
Wiggins, "Blind Tom", 27–28
Wilber, Ken, 90
Williams, Joe, 6–8
Wilson, Colin, 22
Worden, Dr. J. William, 116
Wordsworth, William, 27

X

xenoglossy, 39, 151–53

Y

year, the Platonic, 23
yoga, 131–32

Z

Zeus, 53
Zohar, The, 58, 84
Zoroaster, 128
Zukav, Gary, 21
Zulus, 104

ABOUT THE AUTHOR

JOE FISHER started his writing career as a junior reporter in England. Since then he has worked for newspapers on both sides of the Atlantic, most recently as a feature writer for Toronto's *Sunday Sun*. *The Case for Reincarnation* is his second work of non-fiction following *Predictions* in 1980 (with illustrator Peter Commins). His first novel *Skin Dive* was published in 1977.

After years of globetrotting, Joe Fisher now lives in Toronto.

QUANTITY PURCHASES

EXPLORE THE SPIRITUAL WORLD WITH SHIRLEY MACLAINE AND JESS STERN

Check to see which of these fine titles are missing from your bookshelf:

Titles by Jess Stern:

☐ 26085	EDGAR CAYCE: SLEEPING PROPHET	$4.50
☐ 25150	SOULMATES	$3.95
☐ 26057	YOGA, YOUTH, AND REINCARNATION	$3.95

Titles by Shirley MacLaine:

☐ 05094	DANCING IN THE LIGHT, a Bantam hardcover	$17.95
☐ 25045	OUT ON A LIMB	$4.50
☐ 25234	"DON'T FALL OFF THE MOUNTAIN"	$4.50
☐ 26173	YOU CAN GET THERE FROM HERE	$4.50

Look for them in your bookstore or use the coupon below:

BANTAM NEW AGE BOOKS

Bantam New Age Books are for all those interested in reflecting on life today and life as it may be in the future. This important new imprint features stimulating works in fields from biology and psychology to philosophy and the new physics.

☐	25881	**MAGICAL CHILD MATURES** Joseph C. Pearce	$4.50
☐	25388	**DON'T SHOOT THE DOG** Karen Pryor	$3.95
☐	25344	**SUPERMIND: THE ULTIMATE ENERGY** Barbara B. Brown	$4.95
☐	27044	**CREATIVE VISUALIZATION** Shatki Gawain	$4.50
☐	26076	**MAGICAL CHILD** Joseph Chilton Pearce	$4.50
☐	25748	**ZEN/MOTORCYCLE MAINTENANCE** Robert Pirsig	$4.95
☐	25982	**THE WAY OF THE SHAMAN** Michael Hamer	$4.50
☐	25437	**TO HAVE OR TO BE** Fromm	$4.50
☐	24562	**LIVES OF A CELL** Lewis Thomas	$3.95

Prices and availability subject to change without notice.

IF YOU'VE ENJOYED OTHER BOOKS FROM OUR NEW AGE LIST, WE'RE SURE YOU'LL WANT TO ADD MORE OF THEM TO YOUR COLLECTION

YOUR GUIDES TO THE STARS

Bantam has a wide range of books on Astrology from which to choose. Check to see which titles are missing from your bookshelf.

☐ 26187   LINDA GOODMAN'S SUN $4.95
           SIGNS

☐ 34344   LINDA GOODMAN'S SUN $11.95
           SIGNS

☐ 25747   ROBIN MACNAUGHTON'S $4.50
           SUN SIGN PERSONALITY GUIDE

☐ 25849   SECRETS FROM A $4.95
           STARGAZER'S NOTEBOOK, Smith

Look for them at your bookstore or use the coupon below:

Bantam Books, Inc., Dept. AS, 414 East Golf Road, Des Plaines, Ill. 60016

Please send me the books I have checked above. I am enclosing $_____ (please add $1.50 to cover postage and handling). Send check or money order—no cash or C.O.D.s please.

Mr/Ms _____

Address _____

City/State _____ Zip _____

AS—8/87

Please allow four to six weeks for delivery. This offer expires 2/88. Prices and availability subject to change without notice.

DON'T MISS
THESE CURRENT
Bantam Bestsellers

☐	25800	**THE CIDER HOUSE RULES** John Irving	$4.95
☐	25801	**DARK GODS** T. E. D. Klein	$3.95
☐	26554	**HOLD THE DREAM**	$4.95
		Barbara Taylor Bradford	
☐	26253	**VOICE OF THE HEART**	$4.95
		Barbara Taylor Bradford	
☐	25432	**THE OCTOBER CIRCLE** Robert Littel	$3.95
☐	23667	**NURSE'S STORY** Carol Gino	$3.95
☐	24184	**THE WARLORD** Malcolm Bosse	$3.95
☐	26322	**THE BOURNE SUPREMACY**	$4.95
		Robert Ludlum	
☐	26056	**THE CLEANUP**	$3.95
		John Skipp & Craig Spector	
☐	26140	**WILD MIDNIGHT** Maggie Davis	$3.95
☐	26134	**THE EMBASSY HOUSE** Nicholas Proffit	$4.50
☐	26142	**MATINEE IDOL** Ron Base	$3.95
☐	25625	**A CROWD OF LOVERS** Laddie Marshak	$3.95
☐	26659	**DREAMS & SHADOWS**	$4.50
		Rosemary Simpson	

THE LATEST BOOKS IN THE BANTAM BESTSELLING TRADITION

☐	25891	**THE TWO MRS. GRENVILLES** Dominick Dunne	$4.50
☐	25540	**MOONDUST AND MADNESS** Janelle Taylor	$3.95
☐	25547	**SWEET REASON** Robert Littell	$3.50
☐	25800	**THE CIDER HOUSE RULES** John Irving	$4.95
☐	25675	**BEACHES** Iris Rainer Dart	$3.95
☐	25379	**THE PROUD BREED** Celeste DeBlasis	$4.50
☐	24937	**WILD SWAN** Celeste DeBlasis	$3.95
☐	25692	**SWAN'S CHANCE** Celeste DeBlasis	$4.50
☐	26543	**ACT OF WILL** Barbara Taylor Bradford	$4.95
☐	26534	**A WOMAN OF SUBSTANCE** Barbara Taylor Bradford	$4.50
☐	25418	**FACES** Johanna Kingsley	$4.50
☐	26583	**SCENTS** Johanna Kingsley	$4.50
☐	25709	**ARDENT SPRING** Anthony DiFranco	$3.95
☐	26354	**NEVER LEAVE ME** Margaret Pemberton	$3.95

Prices and availability subject to change without notice.

BANTAM
SHOP·AT·HOME
C·A·T·A·L·O·G

Special Offer
Buy a Bantam Book
for only 50¢.

Now you can have Bantam's catalog filled with hundreds of titles plus take advantage of our unique and exciting bonus book offer. A special offer which gives you the opportunity to purchase a Bantam book for only 50¢. Here's how!

By ordering any five books at the regular price per order, you can also choose any other single book listed (up to a $4.95 value) for just 50¢. Some restrictions do apply, but for further details why not send for Bantam's catalog of titles today!

Just send us your name and address and we will send you a catalog!